WALL SYSTEMS AND SHELVING

BY THE EDITORS OF SUNSET BOOKS AND SUNSET MAGAZINE

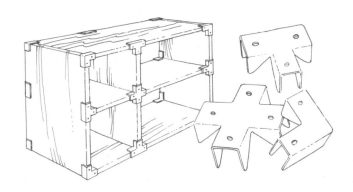

LANE PUBLISHING CO. ● MENLO PARK, CALIFORNIA

We gratefully acknowledge the following individuals and companies for their assistance in gathering the material for this book: Bob Beckstrom, The Owner-Builder Center; Woody Dike, ASLA; Don Fogg, Decoret; Esther H. Riley, ASID; Ray Schenk, Artisans of California; William Thayer, The Workbench; and Ed and Paula Wildanger, Eurodesign, Ltd., Modular Furniture. A special thank-you goes to Hilary Hannon for her assistance in assembling the color section.

Cover: Clad in crisp white enamel, this elegant wall system shows just one of the many combinations of storage features available in commercial units—features you can design into your own project. Designed by Eurodesign, Ltd., Modular Furniture. Photographed by Steve W. Marley. Cover design by Zan Fox.

Editor, Sunset Books: David E. Clark

First printing October 1981

Edited by Scott Fitzgerrell

Contributing Editor
Scott Atkinson

Design
Joe di Chiarro

Illustrations
Mark Pechenik, Bill Oetinger

CONTENTS

BEFORE YOU START

Most of us need more shelving than we have. No matter how many handy cubbyholes, bookcases, or even wall-size shelving systems we may have, our collections have a way of escaping our capacity to organize, store, and display them.

A handy source of ideas and projects, large and small, this book can help you remedy your shelving shortage.

How to use this book

Wall Systems & Shelving has three major divisions. The first section—the one you're reading now—is designed to orient you to the subject; it will help you choose between building and buying your shelving by bringing up a number of the things you should think about before making your decision. It's more than just a matter of economics.

Next, there's a 64-page gallery of ideas and projects, with full-color photos and drawings, beginning on page 8. The gallery is divided into two sections: one on adaptable, movable shelving begins on page 10; the other, on built-in shelving, begins on page 38. In the first section, you'll find a potpourri of commercial, custom-built, and owner-built designs, along with 10 projects you can build yourself. The second section features both custom designs and seven projects designed to spark your imagination and help

you come up with a design for your own situation.

Finally, there's a 24-page chapter on basic woodworking tools, materials, and techniques; it begins on page 72. Here you'll find the answers to questions regarding the best methods of constructing shelves and wall systems.

First, figure your needs

Scan the various rooms in your home. How many areas would gain from additional storage or display shelving? Could your books, plants, and art objects be displayed more effectively? Could the TV, stereo gear, records, and tapes be organized more conveniently? Would a room as big and unbroken as the sea be cozier if subdivided by islands or peninsulas of shelving? This book can show you how.

Regardless of their appearance, all shelves have at least this much in common: they consist of horizontals supported by verticals. Shelves can be supported from the floor, wall, or ceiling, but the basic geometry remains the same.

Appearance isn't everything, especially when you're choosing a shelving design. Before you think too much about what your shelves should look like, consider the following questions:

- **Will it meet your needs?** Think about the size, shape, and weight of the things you'll put in or on the shelves. Consider also whether your needs are likely to change.

- **Permanent or movable?** By attaching shelves to walls or ceilings, you can eliminate the need for shelf backs or other supports, and reduce expenses. A unit built into the wall will also save space. On the other hand, knock-down, modular wall systems offer more versatility, and you can take them with you when you move.

- **Build or buy?** You can save a lot if you build shelves yourself, and this book will show you both permanent and movable shelving projects. But make an honest assessment of your talents, time, tools, and temperament before launching a project: a ready-made commercial unit may suit you better.

Should you build or buy?

Shelving projects are among the easiest you can undertake, and most are considerably less expensive than ready-made units. On the other hand, it's hard for a home craftsperson to achieve the kind of finish and flexibility you'll find in commercial wall systems. Here are some things to think about when deciding which route to take.

Built-ins versus modular wall systems: it's a matter of style, not function. Both the built-in unit (left) and the commercial wall system (right) serve the same purposes. One becomes part of the house; the other can move along with you, adapting as your needs change.

Building your own shelves

When you decide to build a shelving unit, of course, you must first choose the space it will fill. This may be in the middle of a room, against a wall, or even *in* a wall. (Sample projects for all three situations can be found on pages 53, 47, and 60.) Next, consider the following points.

Design fundamentals. The drawing demonstrates some norms for fitting shelving units to people. These are not inflexible rules, but they're generally accepted standards: you can

HIGHEST
SHELF
74"

84"

DESK OR
TABLE
29"

3"

stray from them a little, but try to stay close.

Standard-dimension lumber works well for both shelves and uprights, as do particle board and plywood. Bookshelf space should be a minimum of 9" high and 8" deep for books of average size. Larger volumes may require shelf space 12" high and deep. TV and stereo units usually need 16" to 24" of depth.

Shelf width depends on the load-carrying capacity needed in a particular shelf (see "Basic shelf engineering," below), and the number of things you want to store. If you're building bookshelves, figure 8 to 10 books per running foot of shelf.

Basic shelf engineering. You don't need to be a structural engineer to design and build your own shelves. Still, some fundamental principles should be observed.

The drawing at right shows four basic ways to make a shelf; which one you should choose will depend on the expected load. Always be conservative if you want to avoid a sagging shelf; use the stoutest construction you can.

For light loads (small art objects, stemware, baskets), 1"-thick pine or fir stock up to 32" long works well. For medium loads (books, glasses, some audio gear), you're better off going to 2"-thick lumber at 32" lengths. If you want to stick to 1" stock, shorten the shelf to 24" or 16";

you can also reinforce the shelf edges, as shown.

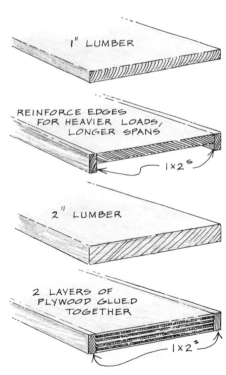

1" LUMBER

REINFORCE EDGES
FOR HEAVIER LOADS,
LONGER SPANS

1×2s

2" LUMBER

2 LAYERS OF
PLYWOOD GLUED
TOGETHER

1×2s

Be especially cautious with heavy loads (wine racks, TVs, large stereo rigs). Use 2" lumber or, even better, a composite shelf made of two layers of plywood with reinforced edges (see drawing above); this will be strong and will not warp or sag unless overloaded. Two-inch-thick shelves can be made 48" long—longer if loads are light to medium.

Uprights can be made from either 1" or 2" lumber. The load-carrying capacity depends more on the strength of the shelf-to-upright connection than on the thickness of the uprights.

The drawing below shows several ways of attaching shelves to uprights. Simple butt joints, glued and nailed, will suffice for light duty; they'll also do for heavier loads if you're using 2" lumber for shelves.

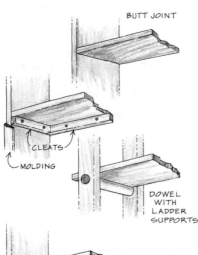

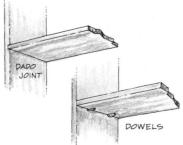

Cleat supports are stronger than butt joints. They can be hidden by a molding, as shown. For extra protection against sagging, a cleat can be installed along the back edge of a shelf when it's mounted against a wall or when a shelf back is used. Of course, this won't be possible with a freestanding shelving unit used as a divider.

Dadoed construction provides strong joints and adds rigidity to backless shelving units. You'll need power tools to cut dado grooves accurately, and once shelves have been glued and nailed in place, their positions can't be changed; you need to plan carefully.

Dowels make handy shelf supports. They can be used between narrow uprights to form a "ladder," as shown, or as pegs to secure a shelf within a cabinet or between side frames.

Most freestanding shelves require support across the back. A ¼" or ⅜" plywood back will secure a unit against sway and rocking. If you intend to place your shelves against a wall and would rather see the wall than a plywood back, fasten the uprights directly to the wall and omit the back (see page 95 for more on fastening to walls).

Shelving hardware. There are many different types of metal fixtures available for shelving (see drawing below). Brackets, braces, and metal angles can be purchased in a wide variety of sizes, shapes, and styles, including ornamental designs. They all add security where a heavy load is to be placed on shelving.

Spade pins and bracket pins, made of metal or plastic, fit in drilled holes in cabinet sides and allow you to change and adjust shelf heights. Dowel pegs do the same thing.

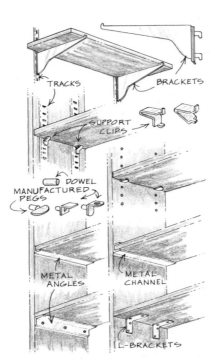

For both adjustability and ease of installation, tracks, brackets, and support clips make a good choice.

Tracks and brackets are really a kind of wall system. The tracks (often called "standards") are attached to the wall; then brackets are locked into place and shelves added. Track-and-clip hardware is designed for installation in cabinet frames, simplifying the building of bookcases and making it possible to adjust the shelves. (See pages 16–17 for complete installation instructions.)

Commercial wall systems

Born in Scandinavia, wall systems have over the years come to be accepted worldwide as sensible, practical, and beautiful. Today, there are dozens of manufacturers and a wide variety of styles to choose from.

It's easy to understand the appeal of the systems idea: cabinets and shelving that you can tailor to your exact needs, yet pack up and take with you when you move—and when you do move, you can retailor the components for your new situation. Some systems even include paneling: in effect, you take your walls with you, too.

Wall systems are either hung on the wall or freestanding. With either type, a world of interchangeable components lies at your disposal.

Most manufacturers offer several types of cabinets, desk units, book and display shelves, record racks, pull-out TV shelves that swivel, even fold-up beds—the list goes on and on.

Years ago, most wall systems tended to look alike, but that's all changed now. One manufacturer alone offers over 200 different modular pieces in 3 kinds of wood and 25 finishes, with 7 kinds of hardware. The result is custom furniture from stock pieces.

The keys to the success of wall systems are their modular design, functional flexibility, ease of installation and movability, and reliability. Here's more on each.

Modular design is fundamental. Let's look at a typical system. Domestic systems are usually based on a 32"-wide module—twice the distance between wall studs in most homes. Wall-mounted supports are anchored to the studs, 32″ apart; shelves and cabinets are sized to span this distance between supports, which is called a *bay*.

Every other measurement in such a typical system is a simple multiple or division of 32″. Shelves will adjust every 2″ vertically, and shelf and cabinet depth will range from 8″ to 24″, in multiples of 4″.

Systems based on other module sizes—24″, for example—are also available. European systems, which are metric, usually correspond pretty closely to domestic modules, but are not interchangeable.

Each manufacturer has a unique way of hanging components on supports, whether wall-mounted or freestanding (see drawing below). For this reason, components cannot be interchanged from one brand to another. You need to stick to one brand.

Wall system components easily adapt to the needs of a family room (left) or child's bedroom (right). The different components are simply rearranged within the system's bays.

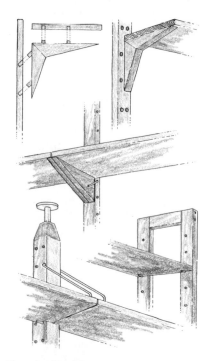

Connections between components differ according to manufacturer; you can't "mix and match" pieces.

Should you need a nonmodular shelf to fill out your wall, most firms will custom-cut shelves to fit. Cabinets are another matter, however; usually these cannot be altered.

Functional flexibility is built into most wall systems. As mentioned, the variety of components, woods, and finishes is prodigious. Some systems allow you to change panels in their doors, making possible such custom touches as fabric inserts that match your drapes, glass panels, or panels painted to match your walls.

The cost as well as the look of your system is flexible, so it's easy to work within a budget. You can buy two supports and a couple of shelves, and your system is launched. (Fill in the empty space with pictures.) Later, as your budget allows, you can add components.

If you stick with the same system in several rooms, you can build up an inventory of pieces that will allow you to recombine units as your needs change.

A small child, for example, might need only a few shelves to begin with. As years go by, the desk unit in the family room (it's getting a bit nicked up by now) might form the nucleus of a study center in the growing child's room, while the family room gets a new unit.

To select system components, start with a list of your needs, then check it against your budget. If you can't afford a cabinet for your stereo, a shelf will do for a while; a deep shelf with a drawer under it can substitute for a full-fledged desk.

Ease of installation is common to all wall systems and is the key to their

movability. Freestanding units are fastened to side frames that sit on the floor; other units may be supported by poles with spring-loaded ends that press against the ceiling to secure the poles in position (see drawing at left).

Wall-hung units hang from supports, usually of hardwood, sometimes of metal, that are anchored to the wall with woodscrews in the studs, expanding anchors, or masonry anchors (see page 95). You must install the supports plumb and spaced exactly according to the system's module size. This is not difficult; it just requires some care (see page 95 for a guide to installation).

If you're mounting a TV, stereo, or electric lights in your wall system, it's often possible to run the necessary wires behind the supports, where they'll be hidden. Some systems have dadoed grooves for this purpose.

Reliability is characteristic of wall systems: because they require close tolerances if they are to work properly, they tend to be made from good-quality materials. If you purchase a good brand from a reliable dealer, you can be assured of a rugged, durable unit.

Wall systems have been on the market for decades now, and most manufacturers have been in business a long time. This stability is good insurance for you. It means you can base your choice primarily on cost, style, and finish.

WALL SYSTEMS & SHELVING

IDEAS • PROJECTS

You'll find the heart of this book in the next 64 pages: ideas and projects for every situation, all designed to set you thinking. Full-color photographs and drawings detail dozens of shelves by both amateur and professional designers.

For your convenience in locating ideas to fit your particular situation, we've divided the chapter into two sections. The first section features adaptable, movable shelves and wall systems. The shelves in this section can be altered and adjusted to suit a variety of needs, and they can be packed up and taken along when moving time comes.

The second section focuses on built-in shelving, custom-designed for particular situations. It isn't likely you'll find an exact duplicate of your situation here, but we think you will find plenty of inspiration and ideas that can be adapted to fit.

Throughout both sections, projects and special features detail particular ideas in greater depth. Again, each project and feature has been chosen with an eye to its breadth of application; you can easily adapt it to suit your own needs.

Projects range in scale and difficulty from small, easy ones that can be built, finished, and mounted in an evening to ambitious ones requiring more time and material—as well as woodworking experience.

The photos on the facing page are your guide to the groupings in the idea and project gallery. Start by looking up the group that most interests you—or just turn the page and start browsing. You may need more shelves than you think.

Space dividers, page 48

Shelves & stairs, page 70

Shelves & fireplaces, page 66

Home electronics, page 62

Space reclaimers, page 54

Tailored shelves, page 40

Movable systems, page 22

Good ideas, page 18

Tracks & brackets, page 12

ADAPTABLE, MOVABLE SHELVES & SYSTEMS

With people increasingly on the move, the need has grown for shelving systems that can tag along. After all, what's the point of spending a lot of time, effort, and money on a nice set of shelves if you must leave them behind when opportunity knocks or greener pastures beckon? The answer, of course, is to take them with you.

This section of our idea and project gallery features designs—from full-scale wall systems to easy, one-night building projects—that will move with you. You'll find instructions for using tracks and brackets (the simplest wall system of all), quick and easy ideas you can adapt to your own needs, and a sample of the many commercial and custom wall systems available today.

Full-color illustrations detail 10 shelving projects you can build, each chosen for simplicity and adaptability. You'll find a range of materials from wood to glass, from doweling to copper tubing and plastic pipe.

The key to them all is adaptability and movability: each can be redesigned or reassembled to meet changing needs, and each can be as mobile as its owner.

Spanning two rooms with differing floor levels, this custom-designed system in clear fir holds crockery in the dining room and books, records, and stereo in the living room. The system is built as a series of boxes, each resting on a 2 by 4 ledger, with plywood backs painted the same color as the wall. The 15"-deep shelves are made from two boards glued together and supported by spade pins in drilled holes. Architects: Pennington & Pennington.

Strikingly handsome, with a high-gloss lacquer-like finish, this freestanding unit can stand against the wall or serve as a room divider. Modular sections containing drawers, acrylic doors, and open shelves house anything and everything. Design: Artisans of California.

VERSATILE TRACKS & BRACKETS

There's no doubt about it: if you're in a hurry, commercial tracks and shelf brackets can be the fastest, most convenient means of mounting a set of shelves. Once the tracks—or standards, as they're often called—are accurately attached to a wall, shelf alignment is automatic and secure. (For complete mounting instructions, see page 16.)

Often, however, the results are less than pleasing to the eye. On these four pages we present proof that this needn't be so. Here are a variety of track and bracket installations—all using widely available hardware—that show how attractive convenience can be.

Track-and-bracket shelves can be fitted to any need and any wall. Here, shelves have been mounted in steps to follow the line of the wall. Dressy brass-finish hardware complements the deep tones of the hardwood. Architect: Marshall Lewis.

Space-efficient buffet fits unobtrusively on small dining room wall without encroaching on floor space. The unit uses four different materials: wood supports and drawers, brass tracks and brackets, glass shelves, and a marble top. Design: Herman Ohme.

Freestanding uprights turn brackets to the wall in this efficient home office; pressure devices secure the uprights in position. Shelves of fir 2 by 10s can carry heavy loads over the long spans shown here. Design: Mara Jones.

Sunlight streams through almost invisible glass shelves that allow indoor plants to merge with greenery outside. Tracks tucked into window frames and white shelf brackets are simple and unobtrusive. Design: Pella Windows.

Lightweight shelves of teak veneer securely bear the family china and crystal, all supported by black-finish tracks and brackets. Tracks rest in dadoes in the wall paneling; shelves are cut from hollow-core doors and faced with teak strips. Architect: Ron Yeo.

Neatly turning the corner between two rooms, track-and-bracket shelves hold cookbooks and utensils on kitchen side, show off display pieces in the dining room.

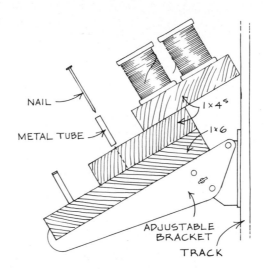

NAIL

METAL TUBE

1×4s

1×6

ADJUSTABLE
BRACKET

TRACK

Tilt-down bracket is the key to this sewing-room shelf. Spools of thread are set on short lengths of metal tubing nailed to an arrangement of staggered boards. The drawing at right shows how it all goes together. Architect: Ron Yeo.

Track systems are now so standard in shelving that they deserve a section of their own. Why the popularity? They're adjustable, easy to install, widely available, and inexpensive.

There are two basic types of track systems: tracks and brackets, and tracks and clips. (Tracks are often called "standards" or "pilasters"—terms vary.)

There are many bracket styles in several finishes (see drawing below). The most common brackets are sized for 8", 10", or 12"-wide lumber, but some systems hold shelves up to 24" wide. Clips come in two designs: one is bent at an angle (gusseted), and the other is flat and sits flush with the track. The gusseted style holds more weight.

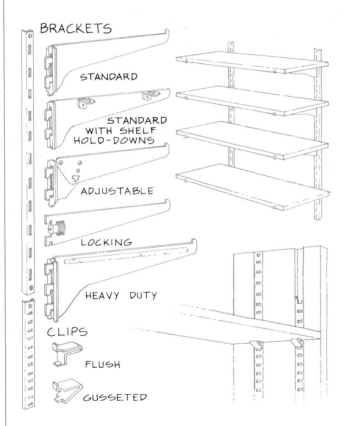

BRACKETS

STANDARD

STANDARD WITH SHELF HOLD-DOWNS

ADJUSTABLE

LOCKING

HEAVY DUTY

CLIPS

FLUSH

GUSSETED

Which type of track should you choose? Generally, tracks and brackets are used with units hung on the wall; tracks and support clips are used inside a cabinet frame. Each type, however, can be used in several ways. The following sections first show you how to install each type, then offer a brief look at some variations.

Mounting tracks and brackets, step-by-step

Tracks and brackets are mounted vertically on the wall; tracks are available from 12" long to ceiling height. Choose your shelf length, then cut shelves (use 1" or 2" lumber) or buy them precut.

To install the units, first decide where the shelves should go. Your tracks should be spaced from 16" to 32" apart, depending on load. Ideally, you should fasten into wall studs with screws. If the wall is made of gypsum wallboard, plaster, or paneling, look for the studs behind; if it's not, you'll need other fasteners (in either case, see page 95 for details). Shelves should extend 4" to 8" beyond the outside tracks.

Place the first track in position, drill a small pilot hole through one screw hole, and drive in a screw. Leave the screw loose so you can move the track. Next, check for plumb with a carpenter's level as shown below and mark along the track's edge for reference. Drill the remaining pilot holes, then install and tighten all screws.

Insert a bracket in the first track, then place a bracket in the matching slot of another track. Lift the second track into position, place a shelf across the brackets—you may need a helper for this—and put a level on the shelf (see below). Level the shelf by moving the track, and mark the track's top and bottom on the wall. Install the second track as you did the first. Add any other tracks in the same way.

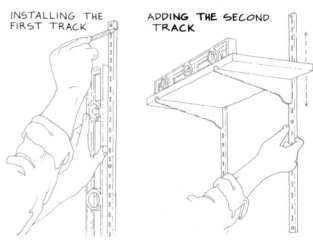

INSTALLING THE FIRST TRACK

ADDING THE SECOND TRACK

Finally, install the brackets. They should lock into place with a slight downward pull; if they don't, seat them with a light hammer tap.

Mounting tracks and support clips, step-by-step

Tracks and clips are normally added to a shelf unit's uprights during assembly. These tracks are shallow, and they're often inset flush with the wood surface.

Whether tracks are inset or not, installation is the same. Measure an inch or two from the edges of each upright, top and bottom, and align the tracks inside these marks. Cut tracks to length, if necessary, but be sure that holes correspond exactly; measure and cut one track, then use it as a pattern for the others.

If you're insetting the tracks, outline them on the boards and remove. The outlines will show you where to cut the necessary grooves, or dadoes, with a table saw or router (see page 87 for details on dadoes). If you're not insetting, leave the tracks in place and attach them with screws—or use the special nails often provided, drilling pilot holes as required.

Finally, attach the clips and add the shelves. If tracks aren't inset, adjust shelf length for clearance, or notch the shelves as shown below.

with the surface of each upright (you'll need power tools). You can also install the uprights and tracks away from the wall with brackets facing inward. This will hide the tracks completely—you'll see only solid wood. Pressure devices (see pages 32 and 35) hold the uprights in position between ceiling and floor.

No power tools? Rather than inset tracks—either for brackets or for clips—hide them behind abutting wood strips, as shown. Choose molding, trim, or lath that closely matches the thickness of the tracks.

A wall of track-and-bracket shelves takes on a built-in look if you add end pieces afterwards. Attach one solid piece of lumber down each side (nail into shelf ends), then finish.

How to dress up—or hide—shelving hardware

Perhaps you'd like a warmer, more custom look than bare shelf hardware provides. Here are several ways to combine the efficiency of standard hardware with the character of custom units.

To hide common brackets partially, recess their tips. Pick the next smallest bracket than the "right" size for your shelf width, and drill ¼"-diameter holes wherever bracket tips will hit shelf bottoms. The tips fit into the holes and out of sight.

Grooved uprights mounted to the wall dress up tracks and brackets. Cut 1 by 4s or similar lumber to track length, then cut dadoes to inset the tracks flush

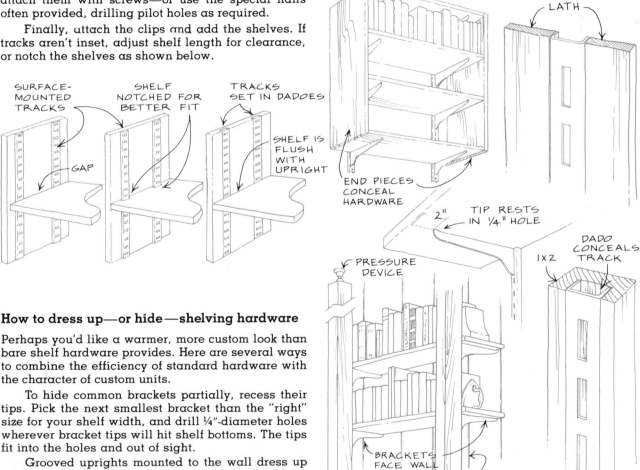

SURFACE-MOUNTED TRACKS

SHELF NOTCHED FOR BETTER FIT

TRACKS SET IN DADOES

GAP

SHELF IS FLUSH WITH UPRIGHT

END PIECES CONCEAL HARDWARE

LATH

2"   TIP RESTS IN ¼" HOLE

PRESSURE DEVICE

DADO CONCEALS TRACK

1X2

BRACKETS FACE WALL

TRACKS ARE HIDDEN

GOOD IDEAS TO USE ANYWHERE

Here's a collection of shelving ideas adaptable to a wide variety of needs. From a simple arrangement of boards and ropes to architect-designed shelves built for custom houses, each set of shelves in this section illustrates a valuable design or construction idea. Each can also be adapted in form and scale to suit your needs, and each can be moved.

Two easy building projects round out this section. Though measurements are given, you can change them to suit your situation.

Take a look at these shelves and projects; perhaps you'll find the inspiration for an original design.

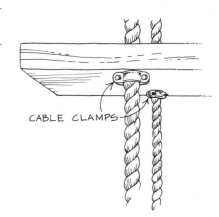

CABLE CLAMPS

Simple innovation: Electrical-cable clamps secure shelves to rope, substituting for knots and making adjustment easy. Design: Mark Jang, Omnidesign.

An organic approach, this shelving system grew with the collection of books and objects it contains. Shelves of 2 by 10 redwood are supported by short lengths of the same wood, by L-brackets fastened to the wall—even by a display case sitting on a lower shelf. A small commercial unit rounds out the assembly. Architect: Ron Yeo.

Tailored to its window, this simple assembly of 1 by 2, 1 by 6, and 1 by 12 pine provides storage and display in potentially wasted space. Nails and glue hold it together; L-brackets brace the corners. Design: Bob Beckstrom.

Simple elegance results when fine hardwood and clean, geometric lines combine. The shelves at right are adaptable in form, scale, and species of wood to nearly any situation. Architects: Buff & Hensman.

Solidly built, these shelves could hardly be simpler—or stronger. Two-inch fir serves as both shelves and uprights; dadoed construction adds strength. Architect: Peter Behn.

PROJECT/**LIGHTWEIGHT HANGING SHELVES**

Here's a basic, portable shelf unit that meets many storage and display needs.

Buy two 10' lengths of fir, pine, or redwood 1 by 8 and cut according to the detail drawing. Shelving tracks, as shown at right, are best set in dadoes (see page 87).

To build, first attach the frame pieces with butt or rabbet joints. Rabbet joints are stronger and only a little more difficult to make (see page 86). Fasten the pieces with glue and woodscrews or finishing nails, and sand and finish as desired (see page 90).

Attach the crosspieces as shown, then drive 1½" woodscrews through them into the wall studs. Design: Williams and Foltz.

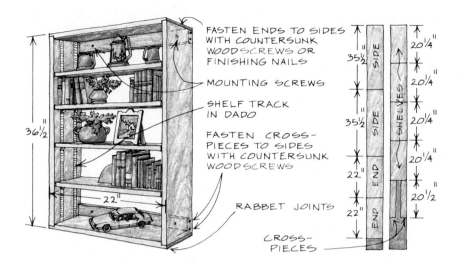

FASTEN ENDS TO SIDES WITH COUNTERSUNK WOODSCREWS OR FINISHING NAILS

MOUNTING SCREWS

SHELF TRACK IN DADO

FASTEN CROSS-PIECES TO SIDES WITH COUNTERSUNK WOODSCREWS

RABBET JOINTS

CROSS-PIECES

PROJECT/**SIMPLE GEOMETRY**

Though these shelves look intricate, they're easy to build.

First, cut all pieces to length: you'll need ten 12", four 36", and four 48" pieces of 1 by 2. Cut four 36"-long 1 by 6s, and rip them to 4½" wide. Mark and cut 45° angles at the ends of four of the 12"-long 1 by 2s, using a combination square to mark. Sand and finish all pieces.

Assemble the side units as shown, using countersunk 2" woodscrews. First, screw the vertical pieces to the 12" diagonals, then add the horizontal shelf supports, checking for square before drilling. Attach the shelves with 1½" woodscrews, spacing outer uprights 32" apart (measure to their centers).

Mount the unit with 3½" woodscrews driven through each corner into wall studs (predrill holes through the outer piece of each upright). Design: Tom Mogensen.

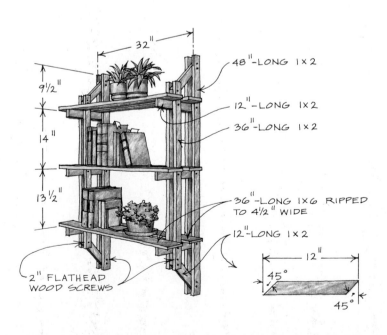

48"-LONG 1 x 2

12"-LONG 1 x 2

36"-LONG 1 x 2

36"-LONG 1 x 6 RIPPED TO 4½" WIDE

12"-LONG 1 x 2

2" FLATHEAD WOOD SCREWS

THE SYSTEMS APPROACH

The idea of wall systems was born in Scandinavia, but it's taken hold in this country too. Dozens of imported and domestic commercial systems are readily available. Today, too, the systems idea—modular components that can be combined and recombined to create custom-fitted storage—has gone beyond the commercial realm and found its way into the home workshop.

In this section, you'll find not only a sampling of ready-to-go commercial systems, but also designs by both amateur and professional craftsmen that apply the systems approach to one-of-a-kind projects. The photos are followed by eight systems-like projects you can adapt to your own needs.

Multipurpose teak wall system shows off its versatility: in addition to bookshelves and tilted magazine shelves, it has drawers, sliding-door cabinets, and glass-door cabinets. Components can be reassembled at will within the three modular bays shown here.

Resplendent in white, this clean, geometric system provides multiple storage in a guest and hobby room. Art supplies sit on adjustable shelves while yarns occupy the record rack. There's still room for the table linens, and guests can use the drawers as a bureau.

Bright as morning, sunny yellow system really puts this wall to work. Its six bays furnish drawer and cabinet space, a magazine shelf, wine rack, niches for art objects, and bookshelves. Not seen behind tilt-down doors: a dry bar and small desk. Design: Eurodesign Modular Furniture.

Solid koa system features a positive interlock between supports and brackets (see drawing). One cabinet frame was left empty, hiding but not restricting a cold-air return grille. Design: Robert Zumwalt.

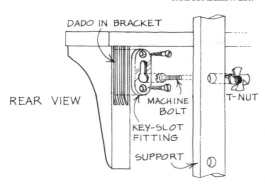

DADO IN BRACKET

REAR VIEW

MACHINE BOLT

T-NUT

KEY-SLOT FITTING

SUPPORT

Combination of features in this wall system provides home office with plenty of readily accessible storage—cabinets, drawers, bookshelves, a magazine rack, and room to hang picture and photos. It all fits in well with traditional desk.

A Scandinavian classic, this system incorporates backing panels that can be continued across an entire wall. The two modules shown here are in rosewood veneer; other finishes are available. Angled dowels fasten shelf brackets to the uprights.

Modular oak étagères can serve as room dividers or, as seen here, as wall systems. All cabinets and shelves are fully adjustable within the freestanding frames.

Like childrens' building blocks, these freestanding white plastic units can be pulled apart and reassembled in different configurations.

Natural quality of this three-piece wicker wall unit complements chairs and floral print used in an indoor garden dining room. Seven feet high to match extra high ceiling, it's also deep enough to hold a full-size TV. The adjustable shelves are supported by small metal pins. Design: Ruth Soforenko.

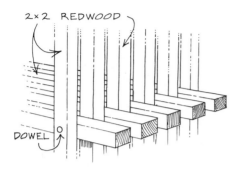

2×2 REDWOOD

DOWEL

Kids' stuff comes in all shapes and sizes, but everything finds its niche in this system. Built of mahogany, the modular unit can be assembled in a number of configurations; it's also collapsible. Design: Robert Darling.

Cat's cradle of redwood 2 by 2s makes a simple, attractive wall system. Connections are easy: hardwood dowels run through drilled holes at all intersections (see drawing). Architect: Pam Seifert.

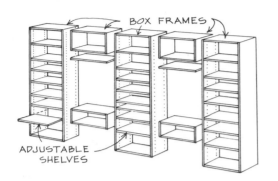

BOX FRAMES

ADJUSTABLE SHELVES

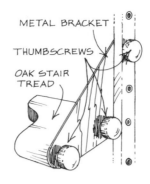

METAL BRACKET

THUMBSCREWS

OAK STAIR TREAD

Oak and chrome combine in this custom shelving unit. Shelves of stair tread stock fasten to chromed uprights with thumbscrews and chromed brackets (see drawing). Architect: Wendell Lovett.

Knock-down unit with a built-in look is really a system of interconnected box frames with adjustable shelves inside; the drawing shows how the pieces fit. Bracket pins set in holes drilled in the box sides provide for shelf adjustment. Design: Don Vandervort.

Shiny chromed wire cages clip together to make a versatile shelving system with a "high-tech" look. Originally designed for industrial and commercial use, they are sturdy enough to hold a TV. The system is also available in black or white.

Wire grids dipped in white vinyl make ideal hobby shelving; they're easy to mount and widely available. Matching rollaround unit at lower right adds flexibility to this darkroom, and small plastic swing-out bins on wall provide miniature "shelving" for small items. Design: Mark Jang, Omnidesign.

Arched tops give this system its flair; design flexibility gives it effectiveness. Open frame gains strength from lap joints (see page 87), while allowing the use of both narrow and wide shelves as needs dictate. Design: Charles Rumwell.

Elegantly simple unit provides a writing surface, cabinet, three drawers, and three half-width shelves hung on the wall in a minimum of space. High gloss, polyester-base paint gives a tough, durable finish. Design: Artisans of California.

PROJECT/**SYSTEM OF PLASTIC PIPE & PLYWOOD**

White PVC pipe gives this unit its sleek look. Use 1″ pipe; for heavy loads, substitute 1″ dowels. The painted ½″ plywood shelves are fully adjustable, resting on supports of 1 by 2 pine that clamp onto the pipes.

For the clamps, cut 22 pieces 12″ long and 24 pieces 28″ long. Drill two ¼″ holes in each pair, as shown. Insert two ¼″ by 2″ carriage bolts and clamp each pair to pieces of ¼″ scrap with wing nuts and washers; drill 1″ holes as indicated. Cut a dozen 16″ by 24″ plywood shelves, sand, and finish with enamel. Make the uprights ¼″ shorter than the ceiling is high.

Assemble the unit as shown, staggering the 16″ and 28″ support clamps. Push the top clamps against the ceiling and tighten the wing nuts; then add the shelves. Design: Don Vandervort.

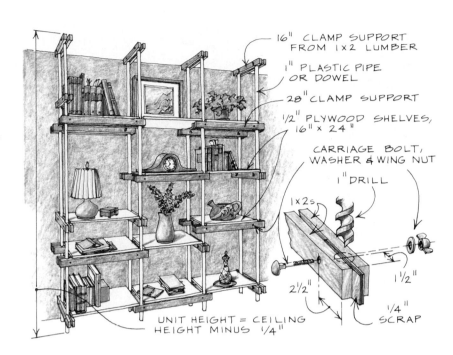

16″ CLAMP SUPPORT FROM 1x2 LUMBER

1″ PLASTIC PIPE OR DOWEL

28″ CLAMP SUPPORT

½″ PLYWOOD SHELVES, 16″ x 24″

CARRIAGE BOLT, WASHER & WING NUT

1″ DRILL

1x2s

1½″

2½″

¼″ SCRAP

UNIT HEIGHT = CEILING HEIGHT MINUS ¼″

PROJECT/**DISPLAY SHELVES OF GLASS & DOWELS**

This unit features ladder uprights and 1″ dowels supporting 12″ by 30″ shelves of ¼″ clear plate glass. Sand and finish before assembly.

Make the ladders of 1 by 4 fir; cut twelve 6′ uprights and fifteen 12″ cross-pieces. Mark the uprights according to the shelf heights you want, sandwich the cross-pieces between them as shown, and glue and clamp.

With a 1″ spade bit, drill through the ladders as shown (see page 83 for drilling tips). Slide 1″ dowels, 66¾″ long, through the ladders. Secure the dowels with 2¼″ brass flathead screws as indicated.

Attach the completed unit to the wall with L-brackets before adding the shelves.

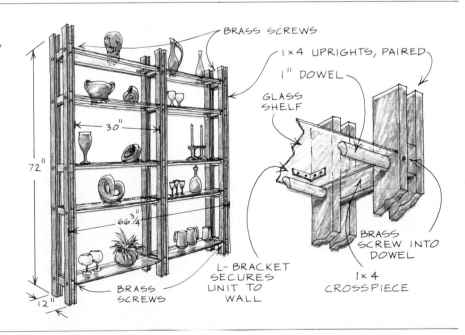

BRASS SCREWS

1x4 UPRIGHTS, PAIRED

1″ DOWEL

GLASS SHELF

30″

72″

66¾″

12″

BRASS SCREWS

L-BRACKET SECURES UNIT TO WALL

BRASS SCREW INTO DOWEL

1x4 CROSSPIECE

Accurate drilling is the only trick to building this self-supporting, adjustable system. It can be set against a wall, or it can function as a room divider, as shown at right.

Clear fir 2 by 3s form the uprights; 2 by 2 cross-supports hold up the shelves. All joints are fixed by removable dowels and pegs.

To build, first cut the six uprights to length—1″ less than ceiling height. Next, cut the remaining pieces. Make shelves from 2 by 12 or 1 by 12 fir or Number 2 ("knotty") pine; length is 24″. The cross-supports are 11¼″-long fir 2 by 2s—you'll need two for every shelf used.

See the drawings at right for details on the arrangement of dowels, pegs, and cross-supports. Dowels 1″ in diameter hold the cross-supports. Cut the dowels 4⅛″ or 5⅝″ long—the longer dowels to hold up two adjoining cross-supports. Finally, cut two ¼″ hardwood dowels 1½″ long, for each section of 1″ dowel.

After the cutting comes the drilling—it's here that special care should be exercised.

Beginning with the six uprights, mark and drill 1″ holes for the dowels to pass through. On each upright, measure 10½″ from one end (the bottom) and mark—in the center. Repeat every 6″ over the length of the piece, and drill (see page 83 for drilling tips).

Refer to the drilling diagrams for the cross-supports and 1″ dowels. Drill two 1″ holes in each cross-support, as shown. Then change the drill bit and drill a ¼″ hole ⅜″ from each end of the 1″ dowels. A homemade device for holding dowels while drilling is shown at right.

Before final assembly, sand and finish the unit as desired. Add a pressure device (one is detailed

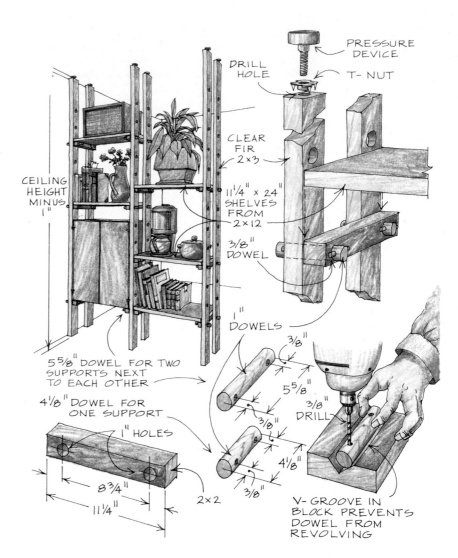

above; another type is shown on page 35) to the top of each upright. These are often sold as levelers for appliances.

Raise the uprights in pairs by first connecting them with cross-supports and dowels, then setting them in position and backing out the pressure devices with a

wrench. Check for plumb (page 95) as you go. Once you've set the first pair in place, use a shelf to space the remaining pairs of uprights.

Simple boxes and cabinets (page 92), set like shelves on the cross-supports, turn the basic unit into a multi-purpose system. Design: Don Vandervort.

PROJECT/**A CLASSIC USING POLES & DOWELS**

For low cost, ease of assembly, and portability, this system is a classic. Adapt the dimensions to your specific needs.

Make the uprights of 1⅜" closet rod and the shelves of 2 by 10 fir. The shelves rest atop ⅜" dowels inserted through the uprights. After cutting the shelves, drill holes as indicated at right. Use a 1⅜" spade bit and drill as cleanly as possible (see page 83 for drilling tips.)

The most exacting task is drilling the ⅜" holes for the dowels. A doweling jig (page 83) or portable drill press will help keep holes straight and accurately centered.

Before assembly, finish the pieces by sanding, staining, and sealing (see page 90). Design: Jerry Jacobson.

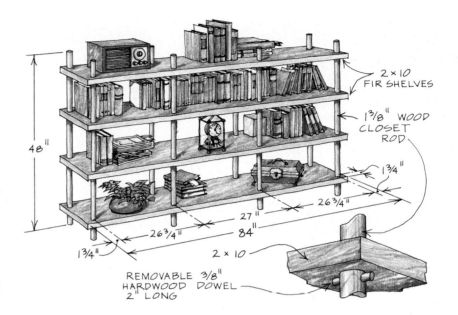

PROJECT/**COPPER TUBING & PLYWOOD "SANDWICH"**

Copper water pipe and threaded rods clamp this system together.

Cut the shelves from ⅝" Finnish plywood (see page 75). Here, they're 12" wide by 8' long. Round the edges with a rasp, router, or sander. Cut the pipes and rods to chosen length with a hacksaw.

The 1¼" pipes sit in recesses ⅛" deep; to cut the recesses, use a 1¼" spade bit and control depth accurately (see page 83). Next, drill ¼" holes through the recesses (for the threaded rod), and sand and finish the shelves (see page 90).

Assemble from the top down, starting with the cap nuts (see drawing) and ending with the nuts at the bottom. A simple wooden frame keeps the rod ends off the floor. Design: William Clark.

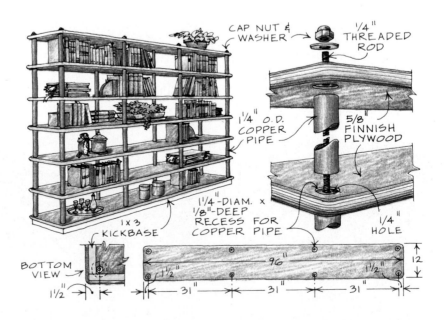

PROJECT/**ELEGANT INTERLOCKING CRATES**

These trim pine boxes interlock to form any number of solid, adaptable units. Build them from kiln-dried 1 by 3s and 1 by 12s, glue, and 4-penny finishing nails.

Cut all pieces and sand before assembly. Glue and nail the first 1 by 3 flush with the sides of the 1 by 12s, as shown. Using another 1 by 3 as a spacer, attach the second 1 by 3, and remove the spacer. Repeat on the other side of the box, staggering the 1 by 3s as shown.

Set nail heads and fill; finish with Danish oil or polyurethane (see page 91). Larger boxes—*exactly* two or three times the dimensions shown—will also interlock smoothly. Design: Roger Flanagan.

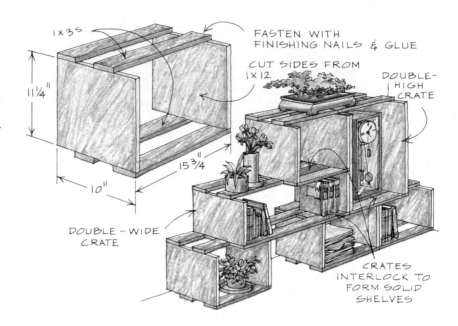

PROJECT/**DISPLAY MODULES**

Streamlined and sturdy, these modular boxes measure 24″ by 24″, but you can size them to meet your needs.

Build them from finished 2 by 12 fir, pine, cedar, or redwood. Rip the rounded edges off the lumber, leaving square edges for clean joints. (You can also have it done at the lumberyard.)

To assemble boxes, use glued butt joints reinforced with ¾″ dowels (see page 88). Round the corners with a rasp or belt sander.

For adjustable shelves, drill holes as shown before assembly. Shelves rest on metal pins and measure 21″ by 11¼″; quarter-inch smoked glass shelves look good.

Sand all surfaces, then seal with Danish oil or polyurethane (see page 91). Design: Rick Morrall.

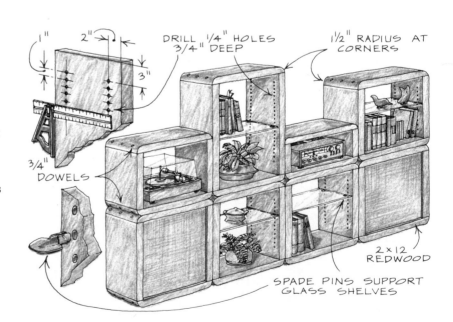

Ladderlike supports, built from fir 2 by 4s and 1⅜″ wooden closet rod, carry the weight of 2 by 10 shelving in this knockdown bookcase. Adjustable pressure devices lock the ladders firmly against the ceiling.

Cut the 2 by 4s two inches shorter than ceiling height—94″ long for a standard 8′ ceiling. Cut the closet rod into rungs 10½″ long. The rungs are recessed ½″ into the ladder uprights at each end; use a 1⅜″ spade bit, and see page 83 for tips on drilling to a precise depth. Fasten the rungs from the outside with 2″ woodscrews; countersink and cover screw heads with cut plugs or small doweling.

The unit illustrated has three ladders set 3′ apart; the shelves rest atop the rungs. Cut the shelves to overlap 2 inches at each end— the weight on the shelves will keep them in place.

With a ½″ bit, drill a straight 3″-deep hole in the top of each 2 by 4, then insert a pressure device like the one pictured at right.

Raise each ladder into position, and back out the pressure device with a wrench until snug. Check each ladder for plumb (page 95) and adjust.

The lower drawing shows a hanging version of shelves on ladders. A solid piece at the top of each ladder attaches to ceiling joists with lag screws; the rest of the unit is the same as the version that stands on the floor. An intermediate ladder should be added if you want shelves more than 5′ long. Architect: Fred Repass.

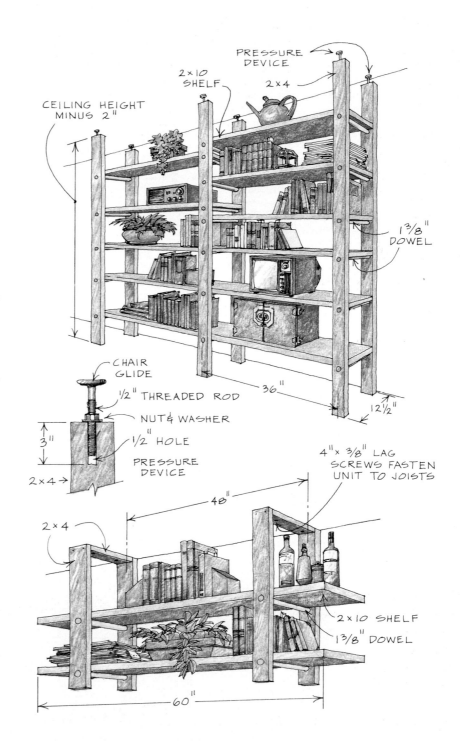

If your only tools are rusted relics from the settling of the West, your workspace is a one-room apartment and the landlord lives downstairs, the thought of building breeds monsters, or there's just no time, this section's for you: quick and easy shelving ideas requiring few—if any—tools and only inexpensive materials. Some of these ideas are classics, others more innovative. Browse through them—then feel free to combine concepts or invent your own. For answers to technical problems, turn to "How-to Basics," beginning on page 73.

Crates and boxes, wooden or plastic, are the simplest of simple shelving ideas: just stack them against a wall. To be fancy, you might sand and finish wooden boxes, or fasten them to a piece of plywood hung by screws driven into wall studs. For more sophisticated box systems you can make, see page 34.

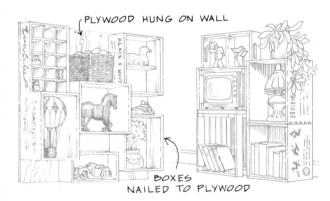

PLYWOOD HUNG ON WALL

BOXES NAILED TO PLYWOOD

Blocks and boards, the student's perennial favorite, are simple systems of boards spaced by bricks, masonry blocks, or anything else rectangular and hard. The shelves can be anything from rough old barnwood to finished 2 by 12s—use stock sizes or cut the boards to length.

Some words of caution: always stack blocks in a straight, even column. If the stack exceeds 5' in

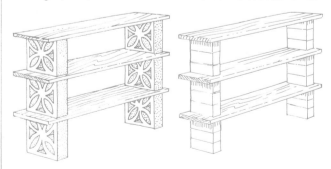

height, "step" the unit in towards the wall or anchor the top shelf to the wall.

Brackets come in a kaleidoscope of styles and finishes; several are shown below. They're the simplest way to anchor individual shelves to a wall.

Brackets with braces or gussets are the strongest. Angle irons can be inverted, as shown, so that a shelf rests inside the bend. Galvanized continuous brackets, normally associated with utility shelves, can do service in living quarters, too. Often used for garage and basement shelving, these brackets usually support three shelves per pair.

Brackets are attached to wall studs, if possible (see page 95 for details on finding studs). Most brackets should be spaced at 24" or 32" intervals, depending on shelf load and stud placement.

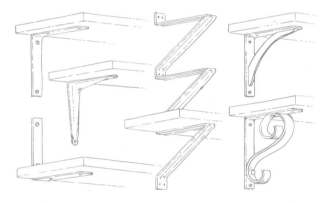

Chimney and drainpipe tiles make self-contained, ready-to-use alcoves. Try square or rectangular chimney tiles to display large books or antiques, and drainpipe tiles for storing wine, letters, or odds and ends. Design a wooden containing frame, or tie tiles together with rope. Chimney and drainpipe tiles come in a variety of lengths. If you need to cut one, use a circular saw with masonry blade, or have it done for you by your supplier.

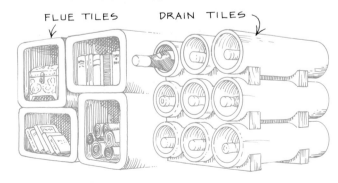

FLUE TILES   DRAIN TILES

Baskets and textiles are effective for storing unwieldy work supplies such as yarn, brushes, tape, and scissors. Baskets or rice scoops straight from the basket shop can be hung on the wall. Sew canvas into pockets and hang them up, or make it into slings and loop them over shelf brackets, as shown.

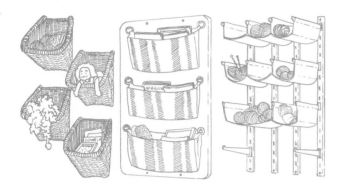

Support clips, metal or plastic, turn shelf boards into an erector set. T-clips, L-clips, and X-clips make reinforced butt joints (you must still cut boards to size, sand, and finish).

Two clips—one each in front and in back—slip over ¾" or ⅝" lumber at each joint, and are locked in place by nailing through prepunched holes. If you use screws to mount the clips, you can take the unit apart for moving or storage. You can also rebuild it in a different form to suit changing needs.

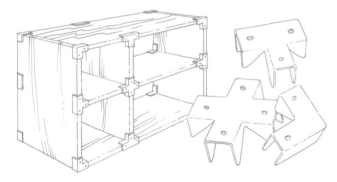

Ropes and chains hold shelves up like playground swings; units hang free or attach to the wall. Drill a hole through each shelf corner, then thread with rope or chain. Rope is knotted (or clamped—see photo, page 18) to secure shelves; chain must be wedged with a wood scrap or secured with a bolt, nut, and washer. Attach each unit to the ceiling (or wall, if you choose—see the same photo) with eye screws; chains connect to the eye screws with S-hooks.

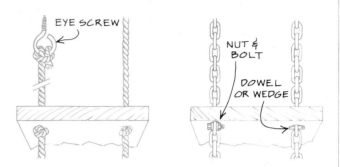

EYE SCREW

NUT & BOLT

DOWEL OR WEDGE

Cleats and ledgers form narrow but secure perches for shelves. Wooden cleats, made of 1 by 2 trim or molding, support shelves spanning a closet, cabinet, or other defined space (see photo, page 59). Cleats along open walls—called ledgers—support the back edges of shelves; front support is still needed. L-shaped aluminum moldings make perfect cleats or ledgers.

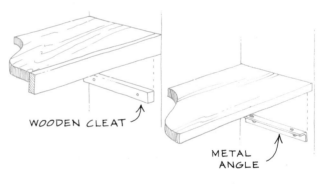

WOODEN CLEAT

METAL ANGLE

Windowsill shelves are simple extensions of the sill itself; just attach a wider board with countersunk woodscrews. For shelves over twice the original sill width, reinforce with brackets or angle irons—whatever window moldings will allow.

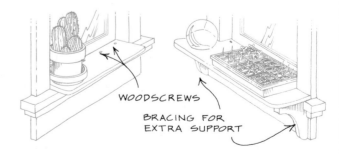

WOODSCREWS

BRACING FOR EXTRA SUPPORT

BUILT-IN SHELVES & WALL SYSTEMS

The luxury of a built-in shelving design is hard to beat. If you're settled at last, it's just this kind of custom touch that can make your dwelling into a real home. Built-ins can be practical, too. How else will you create the perfect niche for that pre-Columbian statue or that huge projection TV?

Here you'll find designs neatly tailored to specific rooms, and designs that tailor rooms to specific needs. There are sections featuring shelves fitted to fireplaces and stairways, shelves that reclaim wasted space, and shelves designed for TV and stereo gear.

The color illustrations show seven building projects, some quite easy, some more complicated. Included are designs for basic built-in shelving, a divider, and shelves that reclaim wasted space. There are a hanging stereo rack and a set of rustic shelves to round out the collection. You'll also find a feature on shelf lighting that will give you tips on highlighting your books and collectibles.

The key to these ideas and projects is permanence. Visually and physically, each becomes part of the room, and each is designed for a custom fit.

No visible means of support: These shelves seem to defy gravity. Actually, they're solidly supported by lag screws driven into wall studs. Heads are cut off screws after installation; with holes in their backs, the shelves simply slide onto the projecting screw ends. Architect: Jerry Smania.

Shelves and wall combine in a sculptural treatment. The wall surface has been brought forward to embrace shelves, cabinets, and a small seat. Clear-finish fir trims the particle board shelves, picking up the look of the cabinets. Architect: C. Douglas Ballon.

SHELVES TAILORED TO THE ROOM

On these pages you'll see how exciting the results can be when talented designers, both amateur and professional, take on the challenge of fitting shelves to a particular room.

Every room presents its own set of constraints—and opportunities. The designs shown here minimize the former and capitalize on the latter.

Sleek shelving design adds a note of elegance to this airy dining room. Cornice molding of stock lumber provides simple counterpoint to the classical molding above. The line is carried over the windows to integrate shelves and room. Architect: Jennifer Clements.

Cozy den gets much of its rustic feeling from built-in shelves of resawn cedar. Depth of shelves is reduced as you move from right to left, with every bit of wall given over to shelving—even the space over the doors. Architect: Ron Yeo.

SHELF UNIT

HOLE PASSES THROUGH BOX TO ALLOW MOUNTING

ROTATING BOX

HARDWOOD DOWELS

DOWEL BOTTOMS OUT IN LOWER HOLE

1/2" GLASS SHELVES REST ON MIRRORS

1/4" MIRROR SECTIONS HELD WITH MASTIC

Versatile room is full of good ideas; two of them—rotating storage boxes and glass-and-mirror shelves in an unused doorway opening—are illustrated above. Boxes rotate inward and desk flips up when the room is used for dining. Full-wall bookshelves are adjustable via bracket pins and drilled holes in shelving uprights. Design: Marc Miyasato.

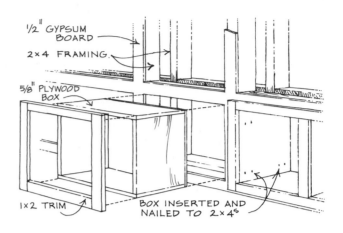

½" GYPSUM BOARD

2×4 FRAMING

⅝" PLYWOOD BOX

1×2 TRIM

BOX INSERTED AND NAILED TO 2×4s

Walls and shelves are one in this bedroom. Extra studs and gypsum board form frames for bed, cabinets, and dark-stained shelves. Extra-deep L-shaped shelves flank the bed. Architect: Ted Tanaka.

Moving the wall out gave these shelves a built-into-the-wall look. The shelves and closet were built as boxes and inserted in rough 2 by 4 framing faced with gypsum board—the drawing shows how it was done. Design: Merg Ross.

Custom-built sculptural oak shelving system slips smoothly along the ceiling line, descending into a long window seat. On the way, it provides a wealth of storage and display. Design: Valerie Montgomery.

You can walk right through these multipurpose shelves and cabinets. At left, extra-deep cabinets house stereo equipment—there's a speaker behind the cloth-faced doors. Shelves adjust individually on standard tracks and support clips. Design: Robert Mentzer, L. W. Grady.

. . . TAILORED SHELVES

Tapered shelves, cut from 1 by 10 lumber, fit into narrow space between window and wall, expand to full width as they move away from it. Painted cornice molding and clear pine edgings emphasize the line. Architect: Jennifer Clements.

Shelves can fit in anywhere; on this wall they attractively frame three windows. Cantilevered from small cleats, the 2 by 10 clear-finish pine shelves are nailed into uprights from the sides. Design: Margy Newman.

Fitting neatly around their posts, these shelves support a collection of house plants and fill the skylit space above a stairwall. Architect: Edward Carson Beall.

Solid oak stair tread, used for both shelves and uprights, frames a sunny breakfast-room window. The nonadjustable shelves sit on nylon spade pins. Architect: Peter Behn.

Teak-edged shelves match twin wardrobes in this library/guest room. Shelves are made of vinyl-clad particle board and adjust on standard shelf tracks and clips. Architects: Buff & Hensman.

What to do with a blank wall? Here's one answer: an attractive system of shelves and display niches built from paired 2 by 8 cedar boards. Special shelves are provided for TV and wine bottles. Adjoining shelves are staggered to allow for easy nailing of the simple butt joints. Design: Bob Halderman.

This basic project illustrates some of the things to think about when designing built-in shelves. Consider it a starting point for your own design.

The unit shown is built with power tools. It combines a basic frame with an optional inset back and adjustable shelves set on commercial tracks and clips; the tracks are installed in dadoes cut in the sides and uprights. You could also use commercial pins or dowels set in drilled holes, or simply fix the shelves in place with nails or cleats.

The unit can be made in almost any size—just be sure you can get it through the door. You can always combine small units to make bigger ones.

Cut the top, bottom, sides, and uprights from 2 by 12 softwood, and make dadoes (see page 87) for the shelf tracks 2″ from the edges of the side pieces and interior uprights before assembling. The optional ⅜″ plywood back can be butted to the finished frame, but should really be set into a ⅜″ by ⅜″ rabbet for the best appearance. Make the rabbet on a table or radial-arm saw (or with a chisel) before assembly, or make it after assembly with a router. Don't forget to rip ⅜″ from the back edge of interior uprights for clearance.

Assemble the basic frame with glue and finishing nails or woodscrews; use a miter clamp or nail a piece of scrap wood across one corner to hold the unit square. When the glue is dry, add the interior uprights, spacing them according to your shelf length (see below).

Build a kickbase, as shown, to elevate the unit and protect the bottom shelf.

Set the unit in place on the kickbase and install the shelf tracks. Several options for shelf construction are shown. One-inch-thick shelves should be limited to a

32″ span—less if you have a lot of heavy books. Two-inch-thick shelves can span as much as 4′, depending on the load they will bear.

Fasten a unit more than 5′ tall to wall studs (see page 95 for directions). Use 3″ woodscrews driven

through the back of the unit; this will keep it from tipping.

Finish by painting or staining, or use a clear finish (see page 91). You can get a professional look by adding trim—molding or 1 by 2 stock—where the unit adjoins the wall or ceiling.

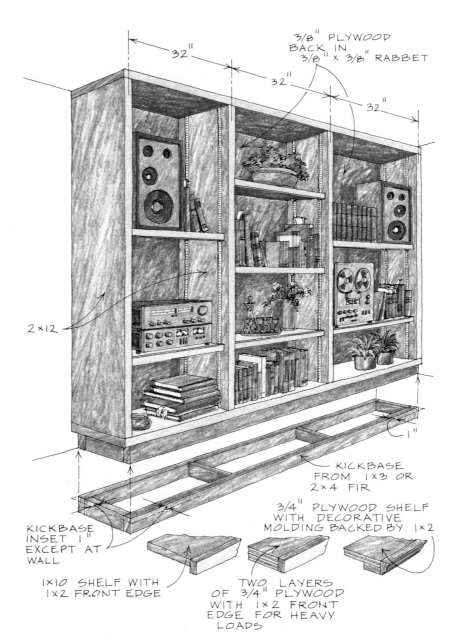

3/8″ PLYWOOD BACK IN 3/8″ × 3/8″ RABBET

32″

32″

32″

2 × 12

KICKBASE INSET 1″ EXCEPT AT WALL

1×10 SHELF WITH 1×2 FRONT EDGE

KICKBASE FROM 1×3 OR 2×4 FIR

3/4″ PLYWOOD SHELF WITH DECORATIVE MOLDING BACKED BY 1×2

TWO LAYERS OF 3/4″ PLYWOOD WITH 1×2 FRONT EDGE FOR HEAVY LOADS

SHELVES THAT DIVIDE SPACE

The shelves shown on the preceding pages were tailored to fit the room. In this section, you'll find shelves that help to tailor the room itself. Some are integral to the design of a new house or remodeling project; others were added to existing rooms.

As you browse through these pages, think of built-in room dividers as potential sites for shelving; think also of shelving systems as potential room dividers. On these pages you'll find examples of both, and a divider project you can build yourself.

Beautifully crafted in teak, this display unit artfully divides hallway and seating area. Light boxes top and bottom illuminate display objects set on glass shelves. Architects: Buff & Hensman.

Living-room shelving forms a bilevel divider and balcony for dining room above. Architect: Jerry Langkammerer.

Angled divider is the major design element in this compact home office. Built of particle board and painted white, it contains a wealth of shelving ideas. On the other side, deep shelves provide more storage—the solid piece seen here just under the telephone backs them up. Design: Rob Super.

Impromptu workspace becomes a neat part of movable room divider when special brackets are used to support a drawing board. Uprights take brackets on both sides, are held under beam with pressure devices.

Shelves fill this pass-through between kitchen and family room. Opposite the kitchen office, the wall opens up with high display shelves acting as a divider between kitchen and hallway. Clear fir is used throughout. Architect: Obie Bowman.

Pass-through divider features glass shelves held in place by tracks and clips. Arrangement is handy: glasses are loaded from kitchen side, unloaded on dining-room side. A single light provides illumination from above. Architect: Jay Fulton.

Cleat-mounted box frames the shelves in this divider between kitchen and dining room. Middle shelves of glass are lit from above; they're held in place by bracket pins. Wooden shelves on either side can be adjusted by moving bracket pins up or down in holes drilled in uprights. Architect: Jerry Smania.

Mirror-backed glass shelves dress up this marble-topped living-dining divider. The mirrors and the windows beyond work to create a play of light in the room. Unit also serves as a buffet for entertaining. Architect: Randy Washington of Vito Cetta & Associates.

Glass display shelves with a solid glass back make a handsome partition wall. Effective in separating rooms acoustically, it preserves the view from both sides. Shelves are supported by small L-brackets. Architect: Daniel Liebermann.

Engineering dictated that these two supports remain when a wall was removed during remodeling. Clad in redwood, they formed this divider-bookcase—an attractive bit of serendipity. Architect: Jim Samuels.

A basic bookcase design can become a combination bookshelf and room divider when the frame is widened and the back removed.

The addition of plywood facings on one or both sides creates the look of a solid wall while leaving separate niches and passthroughs for books and display objects—or just for decoration.

The basic frame, 12¾" wide, is built from ¾" plywood. The unit shown at right is 5' tall by 6' long, but dimensions can easily be altered.

Assemble the top, bottom, and uprights with finishing nails and glue. Shelves rest on adjustable tracks and clips, and are cut from standard 1 by 12 lumber (actual width is 11¼"). Span should not exceed 3'. Shelves are faced with 1 by 2 wood trim along both edges.

Determine the function of each side of the unit, then add ¾" plywood facings where desired. Shelves can be used from both sides or backed by a plywood facing on one side. The facings should be inset flush with the outside frame and uprights. Glue the facings in place; then nail through the uprights into their edges. The shelves' painted 1 by 2 trim will hide the exposed edges of the plywood facings.

Finish the project by filling nail holes, sanding, and painting with enamel (see page 90). After painting, trim frame and uprights (see drawing) with 1 by 2 redwood on both sides. Be sure to finish trim pieces before attaching them. If the unit is over 5' tall, one end of it should be anchored to a wall with long woodscrews, lag screws, or masonry fasteners (see pages 85 and 95). If this isn't possible, concentrate heavy objects in the lower part of the unit, to guard against tipping.

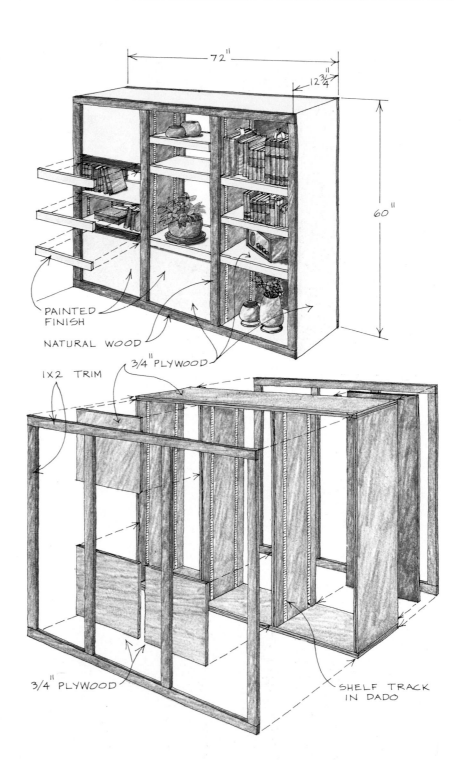

SHELVES THAT RECLAIM SPACE

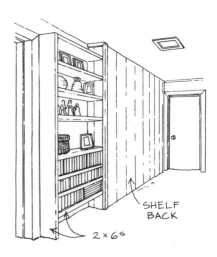

SHELF BACK

2 x 6s

There's a wealth of untapped storage space in most dwellings—odd nooks and crannies, forgotten corners, even the space within the walls. Much of this "lost" space can be "found" again with a creative shelving design.

This section highlights several ideas for reclaiming space that often goes unused. Here are designs that turn wasted space into storage and make efficient centers of activity out of some of the backwaters and byways in every home's traffic patterns. Three easy-to-build projects conclude the section.

Borrowing space from a hallway, these shelves are home to a teenager's menagerie. The drawing shows how the shelf back protrudes on the hallway side. As a bonus, paperback-width shelves make the hallway a miniature home library. Design: Bob Halderman.

Display niche was carved out of potentially wasted space just off the entry hall. Glass shelves supported by lengths of molding are surprisingly strong, yet preserve an airy effect.

Extra-deep wall spaces make room for these sturdy shelves. The arrangement keeps them out of the traffic pattern and makes attractive use of the dining-room wall. Architect: Barry Gittelson.

Taking the idea one step further, these shelves occupy a wall open on both sides. They also incorporate a sliding dictionary shelf, making the unwieldy tome both easy to use and easy to put away. Ball-bearing drawer hardware is the secret to the shelf's easy action. Architect: Saul Wolf.

Preserving the space gained in an attic remodeling dictated that books go in the wall. This logic proved so compelling that the filing cabinet received the same treatment. Architect: James Samuels.

Whatever your shelving or wall system holds—Limoges china, African violets, big band jazz, or more—carefully placed light gives objects a life of their own, making them more accessible to hand and eye. Major light sources include daylight, incandescent bulbs, and fluorescent tubes.

Let the day stream in

Before deciding where to place a shelf, consider how you can make best use of outside light. A window above or next to your shelves can provide display light as well as a view of the garden. A source of daylight across from shelves will give a soft, glare-free glow; closer by, it will accent a particular grouping. Stained-glass panels add an elegant touch.

You may want to highlight windows with a frame of shelving, or plan an extra window or skylight as part of a built-in shelving design (see photos, pages 39 and 44, for examples). Natural light not only cheers a formerly dark room but gives books and collectibles a bright look.

Incandescent lights: most versatile

Standard incandescent bulbs are well equipped for handling shelf-lighting chores. They can hide in ceilings, crane down from walls, slide on tracks, or clamp onto the shelving itself (see drawing below). Because they get hot, keep them away from objects vulnerable to heat.

So-called "downlights" are designed to throw their beams from the ceiling. Because they're recessed, they require attic space for installation. As an alternative, they can be built into light boxes above or below a set of shelves. Glass shelves enhance the play of light from such installations. Cannister lights can be wall or ceiling-mounted and fitted with spot bulbs to dramatize a painting or tape deck, or to light up a vase bursting with flowers. Clamp-on lamps give you freedom to change your mind; you can move them around at will.

Track lighting offers the ultimate in flexibility and ease of installation. You need only a screwdriver to attach the track to ceiling, wall, or—with a miniature edition—under shelves; then you simply twist in fixtures wherever you want them along the track. You'll need to wire in one end of the track; methods vary, so check with your supplier. A caution: components from different brands of track lighting are not interchangeable.

Fluorescent lights: cool and kind to plants

Set aglow by electrified phosphors, fluorescent tubes give 2½ to 3 times the light per watt as incandescent bulbs, and they last 15 to 20 times longer. Place them wherever you want cool, shadowless light: along the lips of shelves, vertically along their sides, recessed along their backs, or hidden in light boxes with translucent tops, bottoms, or sides (see drawing below). To highlight treasures in a uniformly lit display, add incandescent spots to a backdrop of fluorescents.

Although some nonflowering plants will grow under incandescent bulbs, fluorescence is the indoor plant's best friend: fluorescent tubes emit more light in the wavelengths needed for photosynthesis. A combination often used consists of a 40-watt cool white and 40-watt warm white tube set side by side. Special "grow" lamps are also widely available. Keep the tubes glowing for 14 to 16 hours a day; you can connect them to an automatic timer for convenience.

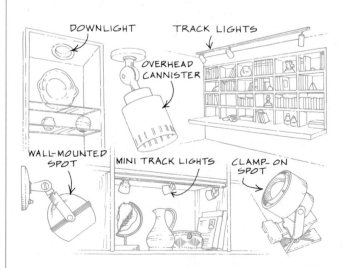

DOWNLIGHT TRACK LIGHTS OVERHEAD CANNISTER WALL-MOUNTED SPOT MINI TRACK LIGHTS CLAMP-ON SPOT

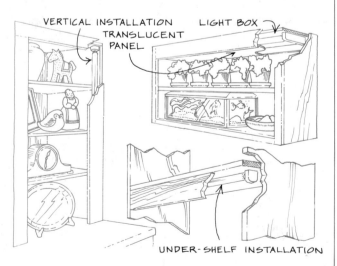

VERTICAL INSTALLATION TRANSLUCENT PANEL LIGHT BOX UNDER-SHELF INSTALLATION

A neat set of oak shelves occupies a forgotten kitchen corner, turning it into a compact, efficient work center. Sliding bookends keep the cookbooks snug against the wall. Design: Tom Keller.

There's room at the top for books in many lofty rooms, and a tall bookcase like this one keeps the space from being wasted. A rolling library ladder ensures that what goes up can still come down.

Shelves can find a home in the most unusual spots. This one—a thick piece of glass—finds support on classical molding and creates a convenient buffet in an odd nook just off the kitchen. Design: Marc Miyasato.

Tailor-made shelves above a writing surface tucked into a porch alcove turn dead space into a functional, attractive kitchen office. Adjustable shelves are faced with 1 by 2 stiffening strips. Design: L. W. Grady.

An expendable closet becomes a neat office with the addition of a desk and a few shelves. Two shelves are supported on ledgers, the rest on tracks and brackets.

The space between interior wall studs is ideal for recessed shelves. Typical 2 by 4 studs allow a recess about 3½" deep—shelves of finished 1 by 4s fit perfectly. Additional depth can be gained by allowing shelves to protrude into the room slightly, as shown at right.

Most all studs are spaced 16" or 24" apart on center, creating opening widths of roughly 14½" or 22½", respectively. The height of the opening is usually limited only by the height of the wall.

To start, locate the studs (see page 95 for instructions) and mark vertical lines on the wall along the inside edges of successive studs. Draw a horizontal line at the height you wish, measuring for level.

Make an exploratory hole 3" or 4" square (a hole this size is not difficult to patch) and check for electrical wires and plumbing; you may need to relocate an opening if these cannot be easily moved. Use a keyhole saw or saber saw to make the opening.

Next, cut along the lines with a handsaw or portable power saw (see pages 79–81). Plaster is best cut with a masonry blade and portable circular saw, and the lath beneath with a crosscut saw. Remove any fireblocking braces between studs.

The shelves are contained in a box frame inserted into the recess. The box at right is built from 1 by 6 pine. Measure the exact width of your opening before cutting boards to length. Two variations on this basic idea are shown at right, below: on the left is a clear-finished wood unit with fixed shelves; on the right is a painted unit with glass shelves.

To assemble the box, glue and nail the two side pieces to the top and bottom, as shown. Next add the shelves: either attach fixed 1 by 6 shelves with glue and nails, or install adjustable tracks and clips for wood or ¼" plate glass shelves.

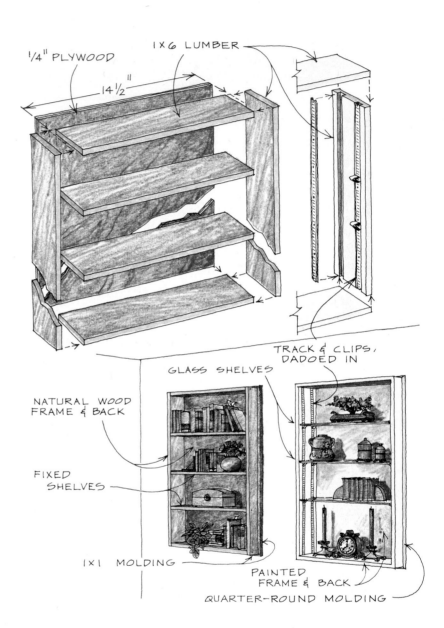

The tracks look best if you install them in dadoes in the sides of the unit. Do this with power tools (see page 87).

If the back of the recess is gypsum wallboard, it can be painted; if not, add a ¼" plywood back to the box, flush with the frame's outside edges.

Attach the unit to the studs with finishing nails. The edges of the recess can be trimmed with molding or small-dimension lumber to conceal rough edges and inaccuracies in the cutout (see drawing).

PROJECT/**EASY, ROPE-HUNG SHELF**

This overhead shelf can go right around the room.

Begin by securely nailing a 1 by 4 ledger to the wall studs. Next, drill finished 1 by 10 or 1 by 12 pine, fir, or redwood boards as shown in the drawing, and drive eye screws into the wall's top plate to match the holes in the boards.

Attach each shelf to the ledger with finishing nails while a helper holds it up. Tie ½" Manila or synthetic rope to an eye screw at one end and string the rope through the shelf and remaining screws.

Check for level (page 95), then tie off the free end. If the rope should stretch, releveling is easy. Architect: Pamela Seifert.

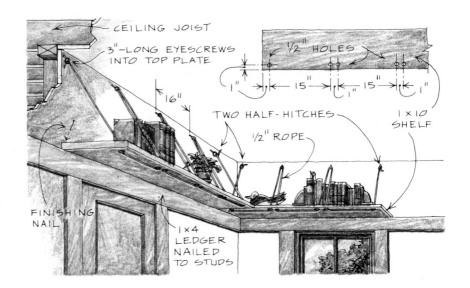

PROJECT/**SHELVES HIGH IN THE HALLWAY**

Long, empty hallways waste space, but are rarely adaptable for storage. Here's an answer: shelves overhead.

Two pine or fir 1 by 4 ledgers run horizontally above door level, supporting plywood shelves that span the hallway. The ledgers can be continued past the shelf as visual elements.

Nail the ledgers through the wall into studs (see page 95). If you can't find the studs, use spreading anchors (page 95).

Next, cut shelves from ¾" plywood—24" wide and as long as the hallway is wide. Attach a 1 by 4 reinforcing piece to each shelf; this strip runs between ledgers.

The weight of objects will keep the shelves in place; but for insurance, drive finishing nails through each shelf into the ledgers. Architect: Howard Schopman.

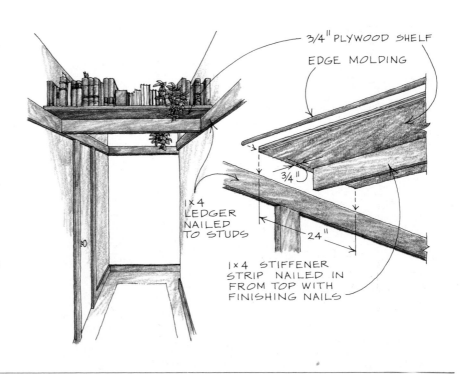

SHELVES FOR HOME ELECTRONICS

The problem with trying to fit a TV or stereo into the average bookcase is that the shelves were designed for books, not for magic boxes that turn your home into a theater or concert hall. Most bookshelves are too lightly built to take the weight of electronic gear, and nearly all are too shallow.

In this section you'll find shelves designed from scratch with TV and stereo gear in mind. They range from a lightly built yet sturdy unit designed for portability to complete built-in home entertainment centers. Finally, there's a building project that combines some of the features of both.

Stereo center designed for an apartment is light enough to move easily, yet ruggedly built. All connections are doweled, and the unit is held tightly in place by homemade pressure devices— lag screws backed out of the uprights against wooden pads set against the ceiling (they're hidden by the trim at top). Design: Mark Bremer.

Good-looking, efficient storage wall uses every inch of space with tailor-made sections for books, records, stereo equipment, and speakers. Narrow drawers are specially designed for tapes. Shelves are ⅝" particle board set on narrow cleats. Their edges are faced with stiffening strips for greatest load-carrying capacity and a more substantial look. Architect: Guy McGinnis.

Dramatic, 24-foot-long wall of cabinets and shelving comfortably houses stereo, records, and even a giant TV screen. Track and clip hardware makes shelves adjustable. Bleach was added to the semi-gloss lacquer finish to retain the attractive light color of the vertical-grain Douglas fir. Architect: Robert C. Peterson.

Audiophile's delight, this home entertainment center has it all. Projection TV takes center stage, flanked by bookshelves and stereo gear. Tape deck and turntable sit atop roll-out shelves and tuck neatly away behind sculpted doors. Design: Gordon Grover.

Varying the depth of a shelving system to accommodate home electronics can be effective. Here, stereo and TV sit in their own "pop-out" unit, while shallower shelves provide for the books and records. Also notable: the built-in wine rack at left. Architect: Woodward Dike.

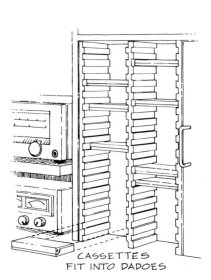

CASSETTES
FIT INTO DADOES

Built-in stereo "closet" houses these symmetrical shelves and cabinets. Dadoed uprights neatly store tape cassettes, yet leave them readily accessible (see drawing above). Architects: Vito Cetta & Associates.

Here's a way to keep stereo gear off the floor, retaining the space beneath for seating or storage. The hanging rack is built primarily of oak 1 by 2s, for a solid hardwood look at minimum expense.

Start by building the three support frames. Cut the 1 by 2s to size, drill ¼" holes in the four longest pieces for the shelf support dowels (see drawing), and join the pieces with end-lap joints (see page 87). (Butt joints—simpler but weaker—may be substituted for end laps.) Fasten the joints with glue and by through-doweling with ¼" dowels (see page 88). Glue in the shelf support dowels. They'll provide support for the long shelf once the three support frames are mounted on the wall.

To build the long shelf, mark and drill ¾" holes in each 6'-long 1 by 2 as shown. See page 83 for tips on drilling these large holes without splitting out the wood on the back side, and be sure to secure the wood to your work surface with clamps. Line up the 1 by 2s and insert the connecting dowels. Adjust spacing, then drill a 1/16" pilot hole and drive a 2-penny (1") finishing nail through each 1 by 2 into the connecting dowels, as shown.

The stereo receiver and turntable shelves are made of ½" plywood set flush inside 1 by 2 frames. (Dimensions shown are typical, but be sure to check the dimensions of your stereo gear first; the design of this unit accommodates various shelf sizes.) Build the frames with butt joints secured by dowels (see drawing). Fasten the plywood in place with 4-penny (1½") finishing nails and glue.

Setting them flush with the backs of the support frames, fasten the stereo shelves in place by countersinking 1" screws through the frame sides into the shelves. The bottom shelf sits flush with the frame bottoms, the second shelf 13½" above.

Fill all screw and nail holes with wood dough, sand lightly, and finish with Danish oil. (Walnut-color Danish oil subdues the pinkish cast of commonly available red oak, giving it a classic "golden oak" look.)

Mount the unit to the ceiling and wall with 4" wood screws driven into studs and joists, or with spreading anchors (page 95). Install the small frame at a distance from the main unit that suits your house framing, and slide in the long shelf. Design: Scott Fitzgerrell.

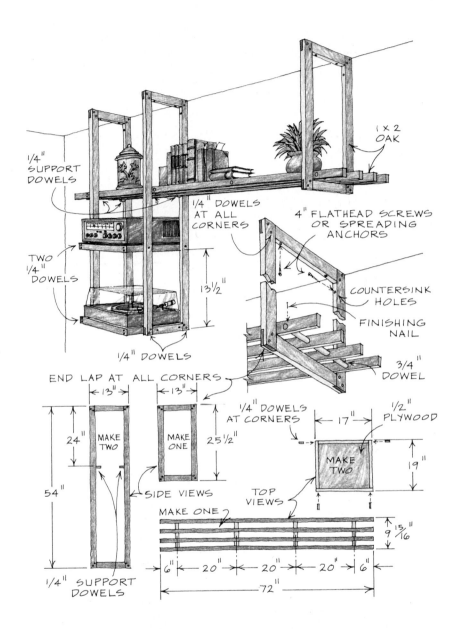

SHELVES & FIREPLACES— NATURAL PARTNERS

Most people would agree there's something awfully nice about the combination of a good book and a cozy fire. It's only natural that bookcases and fireplaces are so often combined.

The next three pages show two basic ideas for pairing shelves and fireplaces. In the first three photos the shelves are used to set off the fireplace and give it prominence. In the second group of photos (on page 68), the mantelpiece is extended into the shelves for an integrated appearance; the overall effect can be rustic or formal, depending on the materials used, but it's always cozy and intimate.

Shelves and fireplace are inset as a unit into the wall of this remodeled family room. An inviting seat ties it all together. Architect: Francis Palms.

Inset bays flank the fireplace in this cleanly designed composition. Shelves of 2 by 10 redwood span the bays without intermediate support, contributing to the uncluttered look. Architect: Peter Behn.

Deep shelves sit in their own niche next to the fireplace, and a raised hearth connects the two elements. Sturdy shelves are made of two layers of ¾″ plywood, edged with 1 by 2 pine. Architect: Don Olsen.

Mantelpiece spans both bookshelves and fireplace, tying them neatly and simply together into a single, integrated whole.

Understated elegance was achieved in this room when fireplace and shelving were tied together. A key touch is the use of small-dimension molding as trim on both. Mirrored shelf backs give a sense of expanded space.

Rough cedar beams wrap the fireplace and extend the mantel as a shelf in this cozy composition of hearth and bookcase. Harmony of materials—the wood tones are echoed in the hand-painted tile—is the key to the effect. Architect: Ron Yeo.

PROJECT/**EASY-TO-BUILD RUSTIC SHELVES**

Rough redwood gives this project its rustic, solid character and makes it a woodsy companion for informal fireplaces. Ease of assembly and simple materials make it even more attractive.

If possible, hand-select your lumber for this project. There's a wide variation in quality at most lumberyards (see page 74), and some pieces of lumber will be drier than others. Select the best and the driest.

Uprights of 2 by 10 lumber, attached to the ceiling with L-brackets, support 1 by 10 redwood shelves on 1"-diameter hardwood dowels.

You should plan to adjust shelf length and thickness to the loads you want the unit to bear. Use 2"-thick lumber for the shelves, or shorten the distance between uprights if you want to store stereo equipment, a large TV, or many heavy books. See page 5 for more information.

To begin, cut uprights, shelves, and dowels to length. The uprights should be ¼" shorter than ceiling height; the shelves shown are 36" long, and dowels measure 3½" each.

Next, mark and drill the holes for the dowels in the uprights. (See the drawing for hole placement; you can adjust these measurements to suit your shelving needs.) Using a 1" bit, drill as straight as possible, and be careful not to splinter the back sides of boards (see page 83 for tips on straight, clean drilling). Tap the dowels into the holes with a mallet, centering each one.

If desired, the rough redwood can now be sanded—just enough to prevent splinters. A satin polyurethane finish will protect the wood while preserving the rough texture.

The uprights can be anchored to wall or ceiling; if the unit is to serve as a room divider, secure up-

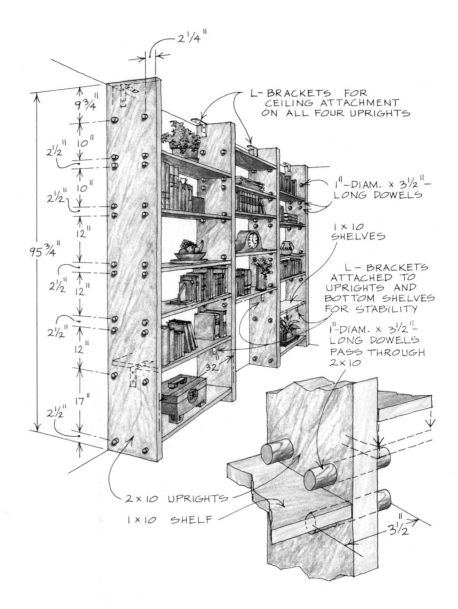

rights to the ceiling. Lift the right upright into place, mark where the L-bracket should be attached to the upright, then lower it to the floor and fasten on the bracket with screws. Now lift the board back into place and mark the L-bracket's position on ceiling or wall. Check for plumb (page 95), then attach—with 2½" flathead woodscrews if you've found a stud or joist,

or with spreading anchors if you haven't (see page 95).

With the first upright in place, space the others down the line (use a shelf to judge spacing), and mount them as you did the first.

If you're fastening the unit to the ceiling, add extra L-brackets to the undersides of lower shelves, as shown, for extra stability. Design: Roger Flanagan.

SHELVES ABOVE & BELOW
THE STAIRS

Stairs run the gamut from the regally elegant to the severely functional. Most fall somewhere between, but whatever their style, all are terrible space wasters.

Stairs take up a lot of useful space—think of a staircase as a large rectangular volume with the stairs running diagonally through it. Above and below this diagonal plane, plenty of room goes begging. Shelves can help reclaim such lost space and make it functional. Here are a few ideas to get you started.

Handy reference center is built into this divider between stairways. Two-inch-thick boards allow for long spans and an uncluttered appearance. Design: Bob Halderman.

Bookshelves climb the stairs, making an otherwise blank wall functional. Uprights are anchored to stairs and ceiling; shelves adjust on standard tracks and support clips. The highest books can be retrieved from a balcony just to the left. Architect: Peter Behn.

Cutaways give a sculptured look to this loft staircase and make room for a sturdy TV shelf and small bookcase. Architect: Marshall Lewis.

Cleanly designed redwood shelves grace a seating nook under the stairs. Shelves match the paneling for a unified look.

Balcony bookcase resulted when the architect used a landing rail for shelving. Natural-finish redwood and white paint tie the design to the rest of the house. Architect: Leason Pomeroy.

HOW-TO BASICS

MATERIALS • TOOLS • TECHNIQUES

This chapter is intended as a basic reference—a sort of "primer" for shelf builders. In it you'll find information on lumber and other materials, tools and how to use them, basic woodworking joints and fasteners, and how to finish and install your project.

The sections in this primer can be read through as a general course of instruction for the beginner or turned to as a reference when specific construction technique problems arise.

The shelf-building process

The sections that follow cover each step in the building of a shelf unit, providing a quick sketch of the entire process.

Choosing your materials. Cost, appearance, and efficiency are the main considerations. Will plywood do, or only the finest hardwood? Do you want a natural finish, or are you painting? Estimate the amounts and grades of all the materials you'll need. This will give you a better sense of what your project will cost.

Materials vary considerably in cost. If you want a clear finish over wood, you'll want lumber that's considerably more expensive than if you're staining or painting. For many purposes, manufactured materials—plywood, hardboard, and particle board—are more economical and more efficient than solid lumber. Acrylic sheets, plastic laminates, or wooden and aluminum moldings can help dress up basic construction.

What about tools? To build shelving you'll have to measure, cut, drill, and fasten. Consider the tools required by each particular design. Will you need tools or techniques beyond your resources for the joints and cuts? It will pay to consider such questions before you start. Remember that the money saved with a do-it-yourself project might pay for a new tool that can go on working for you once the project is finished.

Assembling the parts. Choose joints and fasteners you can handle. Some difficult joints are necessary to certain designs, but usually you can simplify. Once the joints are cut, assembling the parts with nails, screws, bolts, and glue is usually straightforward.

Finishing. You'll need to patch, sand, stain, or paint, and possibly seal the wood (unless you're working with some other material). Then you'll need to apply a finish that's right for the material and for your eye.

What about accessories? Simple cabinetry—boxes, doors, and drawers—can turn a shelf unit into a multipurpose wall system. Wine racks, record dividers, or even a fold-down desk are other possibilities. A section on boxes, doors, and drawers begins on page 92.

Installing your shelves. Will the unit be attached to a solid or hollow wall, a ceiling or floor? You'll need to determine where wall studs and ceiling joists run, choose the appropriate fasteners, level and plumb the unit, and install it securely.

SELECTING YOUR MATERIALS

Undoubtedly the material most often used for shelving, wood is hard to beat for strength, convenience, and price. But wood comes in several forms—primarily solid lumber, plywood, and wood-base products such as particle board—each with its unique strengths and weaknesses.

Your project needn't be all wood, of course. There's plastic in the form of sheets and tubes; metal rods, tubes, extrusions and sheets; and bricks, blocks, rope, chain—the list is limited only by your imagination.

This section details some of the possibilities.

Solid lumber

Lumber is divided into hardwoods and softwoods, terms that refer to the origin of the wood: hardwoods come from deciduous trees, softwoods from conifers. Hardwoods are usually, but not always, harder than softwoods.

Softwoods are much less expensive, easier to tool, and more readily available than hardwoods; hardwoods make more precise joints, hold fasteners, and resist wear better. Because of their low cost and workability, softwoods are the logical choice for most shelf builders; but those who have good woodworking skills and desire subtle grains or colors should consider fine hardwoods.

Lumber grading and sizing

A landslide of terms and distinctions awaits you at the lumberyard. Lumber grades are probably the most confusing.

Lumber of the same species and size is graded on a sliding scale: the top grades are virtually flawless, the bottom grades virtually unusable.

All grading distinctions are based on defects. Decide what you can live with and buy the lowest acceptable grade. If you want a natural finish, buy top lumber. If you plan to paint, buy a lower grade—paint can hide defects.

Softwood grades are especially confusing: the terms used are likely to vary somewhat from one area to another, and even within the same area.

The three main grades of softwoods are Select, Common, and Structural, with up to five subgrades in each of these categories.

A Select, sometimes called "clear," is flawless, knotless wood. Use A or B Select for natural-finish shelving, C and D for painted shelving. Common 1 and 2 are also usable; Number 2 knotty pine is a popular choice for utility shelves. Structural grade is primarily for construction uses, not shelving or cabinetry.

Hardwood grades are based on the number of defects in a given length of wood. The top grade applies to clear wood at least 8' long and 6" wide; quality descends from there.

The best grades are Firsts, Seconds, and a mix of the two called "FAS." Next come Selects, which permit defects on the back, and Common 1 and 2. Below these, the lumber is generally unusable where appearance is important.

Often, clear sections can be cut from lower grades of wood. Sometimes defects appear only on one side, making for some usable pieces where the bad side can be hidden.

Sizing. Lumber is cut into boards, planks (or dimensioned lumber), and timbers. Ordinarily, boards (1" thick by 2 to 12" wide) and planks (2" by up to 12") are used for shelving.

Avoid one potential stumbling block: a 2 by 4 is not actually 2" by 4". Such numbers give the nominal size of the wood; later, when it is finished—planed and dried—at the mill, it is reduced to a smaller size. See the chart below for standard finished dimensions.

Standard Dimensions of Finished Lumber

SIZE TO ORDER	SURFACED (Actual Size)
1 by 2	¾" by 1½"
1 by 3	¾" by 2½"
1 by 4	¾" by 3½"
1 by 6	¾" by 5½"
1 by 8	¾" by 7¼"
1 by 10	¾" by 9¼"
1 by 12	¾" by 11¼"
2 by 3	1½" by 2½"
2 by 4	1½" by 3½"
2 by 6	1½" by 5½"
2 by 8	1½" by 7¼"
2 by 10	1½" by 9¼"
2 by 12	1½" by 11¼"

Thickness of 3" lumber is 2½" and of 4" lumber is 3½".

Most wood used in shelving is finished. Rough wood is often still wet and thus subject to warping. If you want a rough look, think about using resawn pieces or old rough wood that is dry.

Softwood is sold by the linear or running foot and by the board foot. A piece of wood 1" thick by 12" wide by 12" long is equal to 1 board foot. Softwood lengths run from 6' to 20', in 2' increments.

Hardwoods are sometimes sold by the pound. They come in standard thicknesses but random lengths; lumberyards sell what's available.

Other variables

Other variables not always covered by lumber grading are weathering defects, milling, and moisture content.

Always look at the wood you're buying—pieces vary within grades. Sight along the boards for bends; if dimensions are critical, take a tape and measure the pieces. Inspect as many individual pieces as you can.

Weathering defects. The terms crook, bow, cup, and twist refer to board warping. A crook is an edgeline warp, a bow a face warp. Cups are bends across the face; twists are multiple bends (see drawing below).

Grain defects include checks, splits, and shakes. Checks are cracks along the annual growth rings in the wood; splits are checks that go all the way through the piece; and shakes are hollows between the growth rings (see drawing below).

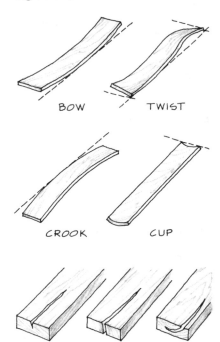

BOW   TWIST

CROOK   CUP

CHECK   SPLIT   SHAKE

Look for general problems such as rotting, insect holes, and pitch pockets (sap reservoirs beneath the surface).

Milling. Of the two ways to cut boards from logs, one results in flat grain, the other in vertical grain (see drawing below). Because flat grain is more likely to warp, choose vertical grain when possible.

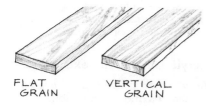

FLAT GRAIN   VERTICAL GRAIN

Moisture content. When wood is milled, it's still "green"—that is, unseasoned. Before it can be used, it must be dried, either by air-drying or kiln-drying. It's important that wood be properly dried because green, wet wood can warp after it's assembled.

Kiln-drying, which reduces moisture content to 8 percent or less, is mandatory for wood that will be used to make fine furniture and cabinetry. For shelves, the choice is more open. But if you use air-dried wood, look for pieces stamped MC-15, meaning that their moisture content is 15 percent or less.

Plywood

Plywood is manufactured lumber, made of thin wood layers (called veneers) glued together. It has several advantages over solid lumber: exceptional strength, resistance to warping, and availability in large sheets. It's also less expensive.

The grain of each veneer in plywood runs perpendicular to those adjacent, so plywood is strong in all directions. An odd number of veneers—three, five, or seven—is used (see drawing).

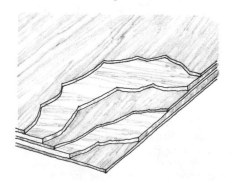

Plywood grading and sizing

Both interior and exterior grade plywoods are available; the difference is the type of glue used to make them. Interior grade is sufficient for shelving that won't be exposed continuously to moisture or temperature change.

Standard plywood sheets are 4' by 8'; some lumberyards sell half or quarter sheets.

Like solid lumber, plywoods are divided into softwoods and hardwoods, according to their face veneers only.

Softwood plywood includes Douglas fir, redwood, and cedar; the latter two are usually sold as house siding.

Softwood plywood is graded on each face separately. Common grades run from A through D. Faces marked A have neatly made repairs and consistent color; D faces have large, unfilled knotholes and splits. B and C grades lie between.

Generally, A faces are suitable for natural finishes, B for stains, and a repaired C face (called "C-Plugged") for painting. If a flawless appearance is important, look for N grade—the top of the line.

Interior plywood comes in several face combinations. A-B and A-D sheets are common, useful, and economical. They work best where only the good side will be visible—where the back will face a wall, for example.

The most common thicknesses for softwood plywood are ¼", ⅜", ½", ⅝", and ¾". Thicker sheets are available but harder to find.

Hardwood plywood, while more expensive than softwood types, is the economical alternative to solid hardwoods. Ash and birch are popular choices, but many other domestic and imported types are available. Specialty-grade veneers are made to order.

Hardwood plywood grading has its own terms; as with softwood plywood, both faces are rated. Premium grade, the best, has well-matched veneers and uniform color; Good grade has less-well-matched veneers; Sound grade is not uniform in color but has no open defects.

Premium grade is suitable for a natural finish—some Good grade

veneers are, too. Good grade looks best when stained, and Sound grade when painted. Grades lower than Sound are generally not used for shelving.

Hardwood plywood thicknesses include ⅛", ³⁄₁₆", ¼", ⅜", ½", ⅝", ¾", and 1".

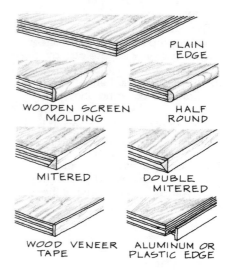

PLAIN EDGE

WOODEN SCREEN MOLDING   HALF ROUND

MITERED   DOUBLE MITERED

WOOD VENEER TAPE   ALUMINUM OR PLASTIC EDGE

Some grades of plywood may have voids in the inner veneers, and these can be unsightly if the edges are to be exposed. If the appearance of plywood edges presents a problem, you can cover them with paint, veneer, or molding. Another solution is to buy solid-core sheets. Made of face veneers glued to a solid core, this kind of plywood has easily worked edges and holds fasteners better than veneer-core plywood.

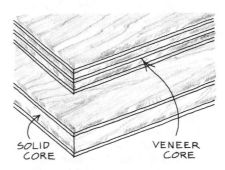

SOLID CORE   VENEER CORE

To guarantee uniform veneer quality, look for cabinet grade plywood. You might also try Finnish plywood, a birch plywood made up of many very thin, solid veneers. With this material, edges left exposed have a handsome, finished appearance (see page 33).

Hardwood veneers. Many types of hardwood are available in very thin veneers. Like plastic laminate, veneer is used to dress up particle board and inexpensive grades of wood as an economical alternative to expensive solid hardwood or hardwood plywood. Some exotic woods are available only in veneers.

Standard widths run from 8″ to 24″, in lengths up to 8′. Flexible veneer sheets up to 4′ wide are also available; they greatly simplify veneering large surfaces. Veneer "tape" is available for covering ends and edges.

A word of caution: veneering is an exacting, often difficult task (see page 90 for instructions); if the hardwood you want is available as plywood or solid wood, that's probably your best bet in spite of the expense.

Hardboard

Hardboard is a wood product made by reducing wood chips to fibers, then bonding the fibers back together with their natural adhesive—lignin.

Hardboard is harder, denser, and cheaper than plywood. Like plywood, it comes in 4′ by 8′ sheets.

An artificial product, hardboard has no grain and is strong in all directions. Its smooth, dense surface takes paint well.

Hardboard comes in many textures, patterns, and colors. It usually is smooth on both sides, or has a meshlike texture on the back. There are two main types: standard and tempered, the latter treated for strength and moisture resistance. Hardboard is usually available only in ⅛″ and ¼″ thicknesses.

Hardboard doesn't hold fasteners well; it's usually necessary to drive them through it into solid wood.

Hardboard also has a tendency to swell and contract with changing humidity. It's easy to cut and shape, but dulls tools rapidly.

In shelving, the main uses for hardboard include backing, doors, and drawer bottoms. Perforated hardboard, or pegboard, is often used with metal pegs, hooks, and brackets for hang-up storage.

Particle board (chipboard)

Made from particles of wood impregnated with glue and pressed into sheets, particle board has a speckled appearance, in contrast to the smooth look of hardboard. Even so, it has a smoother surface than standard Douglas fir plywood. Sheet size is 4′ by 8′; thicknesses run from ¼″ to ¾″. It is available in both interior and exterior varieties. Standard tools are used to work particle board, but cutting tools dull quickly.

One of the least expensive building materials, particle board is an excellent choice under certain circumstances. It's especially suitable when you're planning an opaque finish, when its heavy weight is unimportant, and when you won't need to screw or nail into it—with its brittle composition, particle board doesn't hold screws and nails well, though you can nail or screw through it into wood. Glue and bolts work best.

Particle board makes good low-cost painted shelving. You can smooth its pitted edges by using a paste filler and sanding. Don't finish particle board with water-base paint; the water tends to soak in, causing the grain to rise. Don't use particle board for long shelves (over 3½′) without intermediate support: longer pieces tend to sag under their own weight. For shorter shelves, it's excellent.

Easy-to-use plastics

Two plastics are often used in cabinetmaking: plastic laminate and acrylic plastic. Laminate is used most often, covering hundreds of thousands of kitchen cabinet and bathroom vanity counters. Acrylic plastic is popular for sliding cabinet doors; extrusions—tubes and other shapes—can be used as supports and for trim.

Plastic laminate

A veneer applied to plywood or particle board to decorate or protect the wood beneath, plastic laminate is itself a sandwich of veneers— several layers of thin paper treated with synthetic resins. The layer next to the top is the decorative layer, printed with color, pattern, or texture. The top layer is a clear coating that makes the laminate resistant to scratches, stains, moisture, and heat.

Plastic laminate comes in various thicknesses, intended for top, side, or back surfaces. You'll find instructions for its use on page 90.

Acrylic sheets and extrusions

Acrylic plastic sheets can be used for shelves and sliding cabinet doors, acrylic tubes and moldings for shelving uprights. Acrylic comes in many colors as well as clear. Though the surface scratches easily, it can be buffed smooth with special buffing compounds. Transparent acrylic shows scratches most clearly.

Acrylic plastic can be sawed, drilled, and bent. You'll find instructions for working with it on page 90.

Wooden and metal moldings

Wooden moldings—narrow wooden strips milled in many shapes and styles—lend a finished look to shelving (see drawing below). Popular for dressing up plain shelves and hiding fasteners and less-than-perfect joints, moldings are also a good choice for covering exposed plywood edges.

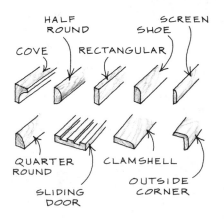

Aluminum moldings come in many shapes and sizes (see drawing above right). They're as useful as their wooden counterparts for finishing rough wood edges, and they look good with acrylics and laminates.

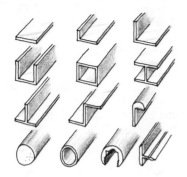

Dowels and rounds

These cylindrical lengths of wood are important in several ways to wall systems and shelving. Dowels are made from hardwoods—oak, maple, or mahogany—and designed for reinforcing joints and fasteners; but they also make excellent support pegs for shelves. Diameters run from ⅛" to 1" in lengths of 3' or 4'. Rounds—pine or fir dowels in diameters up to 1¾" and lengths to 20'—can be used as shelving uprights.

Other materials

Wall systems and shelf units usually consist of some combination of shelves and uprights. Shelves are horizontal display or storage surfaces; uprights are vertical elements that hold the shelves in place.

Any material that can support the necessary weight without breaking or bending can be a shelf, and anything that keeps shelves from spilling, swinging, or swaying can be an upright.

Many materials not normally associated with interior woodworking can be used for shelves and uprights. The possibilities are endless—check hardware stores, flea markets, and your garage for creative ideas. Here are some examples of what you may find.

Chain. Remember playground swings? Think of the seat as a shelf, and the chains as uprights. Thick chains fastened securely to the ceiling can hold shelves stably and attractively. The more weight on them, the less they'll swing. For extra stability, though, tie the chains to the wall behind.

Ropes can serve the same function as chains; try Manila hemp, dacron, or nylon—the thicker the better. Natural Manila tends to stretch less than nylon; low-stretch synthetic rope is available at boat chandleries.

Bricks and cinder blocks have become a popular choice for holding up loose boards, from finished pine to old barn wood. Brick and board systems can be stacked up indefinitely, but watch out for two hazards: sway and excessive weight. A tall stack should be placed against a wall, not left freestanding. Bricks should be carefully centered one above the other.

Boxes and crates made of wood or plastic can become ready-made shelves. Stack them or attach them to the wall. Old produce crates and wine boxes work well, or you can build your own.

Metal and plastic pipe can be fashioned into uprights and horizontal supports for shelves. Plastic pipe (PVC) is easier to work with; galvanized metal pipe is stronger. Both are available with many types of couplings. When buying PVC, ask for "thickwall" tubing at least 1" in diameter or stouter.

Threaded rods, long bolt shafts without heads, can become instant uprights. Drill holes in shelving boards and run threaded rods through the holes, using nuts and washers to clamp the boards in place. Special couplings are available to tie rods together for greater lengths.

TOOLS & THEIR USES

Tools for measuring and marking, cutting, shaping, drilling, and fastening—this section outlines basic techniques for using them to create shelving of every kind. Here you'll find descriptions of the basic hand tools and their powered counterparts, with instructions on using them safely and effectively.

Hand tools or power tools?

Woodworking principles haven't changed much over the years, but technology has. Faster, more precise, and more expensive ways have been found to do basic tasks.

When considering tools, think of the three basic types: hand tools, portable power tools, and stationary power tools.

Most tools perform some variation of two main functions: cutting and shaping. A simple shelf supported by wall brackets doesn't demand precise tooling, but some joints must be very accurate, and with hand tools, this requires time and experience. That's where power tools are helpful.

In general, stationary power tools are fastest and most accurate—hand tools less so. But the big machines are quite a bit more expensive: a good radial-arm saw costs about 20 times what a good handsaw costs.

Portable power tools may be your best bet. When guided effectively, they are nearly as accurate as stationary power tools—and more mobile. Some very good models are not much more expensive than fine hand tools.

For the kinds of projects covered in this book, hand tools are normally adequate, if used with the basic skill that anyone can acquire. But for greater ease and precision, consider the portable power tools; they are an intelligent compromise between efficiency and cost.

It's best to buy a few good tools rather than many cheap ones—a rule that applies to all three categories of tools. Ask knowledgeable friends, professionals, or hardware dealers for recommendations. Buying good tools will save you money in the long run.

Safety

Always remember these safety tips before using tools:
- Work on a steady surface, with

plenty of operating room and good lighting.

● Read all instructions and safety precautions that accompany a new tool. Ask someone knowledgeable, such as your dealer, for instructions on its use.

● Wear safety goggles when using power tools, and keep fingers well away from any moving blade.

● Unplug any power tool not in immediate use.

● "Double-insulated" tools have extra protection against electrical shock built in, so they don't require three-prong grounding plugs. But if your tool isn't double-insulated, and you adapt it to an ungrounded (two-prong) wall outlet, you're not protected.

Try to find a place to work where, if you leave things lying about (as you're bound to do), they won't become a hazard. A workbench with room for storing tools as well as working is ideal, but any open area will do. Pick an out-of-the-way spot where you can spread things out, where glue can set up and varnish dry.

An uncrowded horizontal surface, some type of sawhorse, and a woodworking vise will save untold aggravation. By helping you to hold the work steady, they will also contribute to better results and safer working conditions.

Measuring and marking

Once you've chosen your materials, you'll have to measure and mark them for cutting; for this you'll need a measuring tool, a straightedge, and something to mark with. The ultimate success or failure of your project can be determined at this stage. Here's how to ensure success.

How to use measuring tools

Getting a project off on the right foot depends on careful measuring. Tight-fitting joinery for fine cabinets demands measuring and cutting to within 1/32" or 1/64". Less critical bookshelf boards and pieces can be cut to within 1/16". For rough measuring, you can use a wooden yardstick or ruler; for more precise work, use a metal tape measure, a metal yardstick, or a square's blade. Whenever

possible during construction, use one material to transfer measurements to another (see drawing below). No matter what tools you use, measure twice and cut only once.

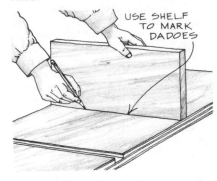

Steel tape measure. For longer measurements, use a flexible steel tape—the longer and wider the better.

A tape measure's end hook should be riveted loosely, so that it will adjust for precise "inside" and "outside" measurements. The case should be an even 2 or 3 inches long for accurate inside measurements (see drawing below). Most tapes are marked at 1/16" increments, accurate enough for shelving.

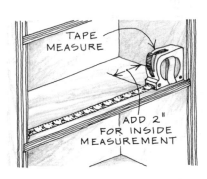

The bench rule is a standard steel or wooden rule 1' to 2' long. It usually has increments of 1/8" marked on one side and 1/16" on the other. The bench rule is convenient for short measurements, and it provides a firm

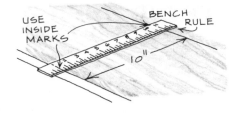

straightedge to mark against. For greatest accuracy, measure from an "inside" mark, not the end.

Combination square. The blade of a combination square excels for making precise, short measurements; the versatility of this tool offers several bonuses. Shown below are some of the jobs it can do. If you don't own a combination square, consider buying one. It could be one of your most useful tools.

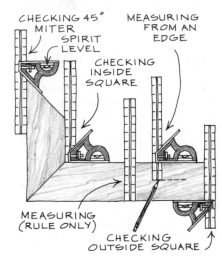

Carpenter's square. Normally a carpenter's framing and planning tool, the 16" by 24" square is great for laying out lines and checking for square when a combination square is too small.

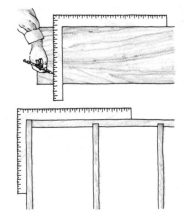

Sliding T-bevel. For marking 90° or 45° angles across a board, use a combination square. For other angles between 0° and 180°, use an adjustable T-bevel, commonly used for transferring fixed angles from piece to piece. Its blade can be set for any angle with the aid of a protractor. Some T-bevels have angles marked on the face.

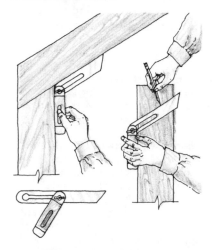

Compass or wing dividers. A simple, schoolroom compass works for limited measuring jobs; it also draws circles or arcs as discussed under "Marking lines accurately," below. Wing dividers are more precise but cost more (they have a knurled screw that holds the legs in place). Use them to transfer small measurements or to step off equal marks.

For large-scale curves and circles, tack one end of a thin board or yardstick to the material, hold a pencil against the board at the desired radius, and pivot.

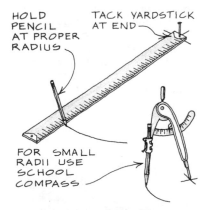

HOLD PENCIL AT PROPER RADIUS

TACK YARDSTICK AT END

FOR SMALL RADII USE SCHOOL COMPASS

Marking lines accurately

Laying out most projects will require drawing lines—some straight, some curved, some at a particular angle. The first tool you'll need for this is a pointed scribe, a sharp utility knife, or a good sharp pencil. A scribe or knife marks a more precise line, but

the mark it leaves cannot be erased; a pencil line can.

Some marking tips: For accurate lines and markings, tilt the pencil so the lead is as flush as possible against the straightedge (see drawing below). When measuring a

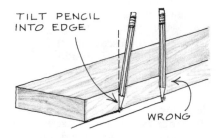

TILT PENCIL INTO EDGE

WRONG

board for a cut, first mark, then draw the line so the thickness of the line lies outside the measured area (on the "waste" side). To transfer irregular outlines to a board, use wing dividers or a compass, as shown in the drawing below.

Sawing and shaping

Because proper cuts are so crucial to a project's success, it's worth investing time and patience in cutting carefully and accurately.

Most lumberyards do cutting for a small fee. Find out which lumberyards in your area offer this service and at what cost; it can really pay off, especially when you have a 4' by 8' sheet of plywood to cart home and cut up. If you ask the dealer to make some cuts, plan your cutting diagrams so he'll make the longest ones. Be sure to specify whether or not the measurements must be exact.

Sawing isn't the only way to cut into wood. Other cutting processes discussed in this section include

drilling holes, chiseling, planing, and abrading. The information on sawing is divided into two main sections: cutting straight lines and cutting curves. Though these two jobs usually require different tools, all sawing jobs have certain traits in common.

The number of teeth per inch along a saw blade determines the kind of cut it makes. The fewer the teeth, the rougher the cut—many teeth make a smooth cut. The best handsaws for cutting plywood and finish work have 8 to 12 teeth per inch. There are various types of plywood-cutting blades for doing this kind of work with power saws.

Where saw teeth exit, wood will tend to splinter and break away. You can minimize this if you know whether to turn the good side of the wood up or down. The side of the wood that tends to break away will depend on the saw you use. Some have upward-cutting blades; others cut downward. Look to see what direction the teeth are pointed—that is, the direction they cut into the wood. Cut with the good side up when using a handsaw, table saw, or radial-arm saw. If you use a portable circular saw or saber saw, cut with the good side down.

Don't forget to support both halves of the piece you're cutting. Otherwise, the saw will bind and, as you near the end of the cut, the unsupported piece will break away. If the saw binds anyway, stick a screwdriver or nail in the end of the cut to spread it open.

Sawing straight lines

The simplest and least expensive tool for sawing straight lines is the handsaw. Two basic types are available: the ripsaw and the crosscut saw. The ripsaw is made to cut only along the grain of the wood. Choose the crosscut saw instead; it's better for general cutting.

Other saws designed for cutting straight lines include the backsaw, power circular saw, radial-arm saw, and the table saw. The saber saw (also called a portable jigsaw) is versatile enough to cut both straight and curved lines accurately.

Crosscut saw. This saw can do almost any straight woodcutting job. If you don't have a power saw, the crosscut saw will be the most important saw in your tool collection for this book's projects.

The length of crosscut blades varies from about 20" to 26". A 26" blade is a good choice. Crosscut saws do about 75 percent of their cutting on the downstroke and 25 percent on the upstroke.

How to saw straight lines? The secret is to use a guide. Clamp a straight piece of scrap wood directly behind the line to be cut and use a crosscut saw held at an angle to the work surface.

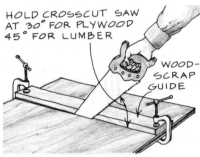

HOLD CROSSCUT SAW AT 30° FOR PLYWOOD 45° FOR LUMBER

WOOD-SCRAP GUIDE

Start a cut by slowly drawing the saw *up* a few times to make a notch or kerf. If you make a full kerf about ½" into the far edge of the board, it will help guide the blade for the remainder of the cut. For clean, straight cuts with a minimum of effort, grasp the handle firmly and cut as shown above, your forearm in line with the teeth.

Backsaw. Used for finish work, a backsaw cuts straight lines precisely. If you won't be doing much critical finish cutting, you can probably get along without one. Rectangular in shape, the fine-cutting backsaw derives its name from a metal reinforcing strip that runs along the spine of the blade to keep it from bowing.

The backsaw shown below is being used in a wooden miter box to cut a piece of molding at an accurate angle. Backsaws are available

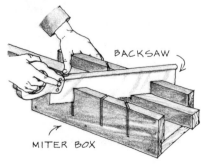

BACKSAW

MITER BOX

in lengths from 12" to 28", but for the home workshop a 12" or 14" saw is best. Twelve teeth per inch is right unless you're doing very fine work, in which case a dovetail backsaw works best. Dovetail saws have shorter, thinner blades with finer teeth, and their handles are straight—shaped much like the handles of screwdrivers.

Unlike the crosscut saw, the backsaw is held so its blade is parallel to the cutting surface when you're sawing.

Hacksaw. Designed for materials other than wood, the hacksaw is good for cutting plastic and metal pipe and threaded rod.

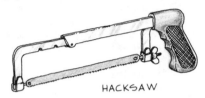

HACKSAW

Power portable circular saw. Though the portable circular saw can probably cut about five times faster than a handsaw, it can be a dangerous tool and requires extreme caution. Unless you plan to do a lot of cutting in the future and are willing to learn how to handle one of these saws, don't rush out and buy one.

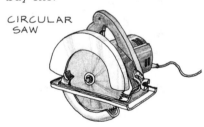

CIRCULAR SAW

As a general rule, power tools do faster and more precise work than hand tools, after you've learned to use them properly. But a tool such as the power circular saw feels heavy, bulky, and hard to manage at first. To assist in cutting long, straight lines with one, use a guide like the one shown above left.

Remember, the blade of a circular saw cuts upward. To avoid splintering on the good side of materials, cut them with the good side down. Set the blade so the teeth protrude just through the wood's surface.

A good way to cut large sheets is to lay two or three scrap 2 by 4s

across two sawhorses and adjust the saw so the blade will cut through your material and only partially through the scraps. By supporting the piece during the cutting, the 2 by 4s will make it more manageable.

Sized according to blade diameter, circular saws range from 5½" to 10", and there are dozens of blade types. A 7" to 7½" saw with a combination blade (designed to do both crosscut and rip sawing) works best for most home woodworking and cabinetmaking jobs.

Saber saw (jigsaw). Though used chiefly for cutting curves, the saber saw also cuts surprisingly straight lines when used with a guide. A guide is usually furnished with the saw for making parallel cuts a short distance from a board's edge. For cutting across panels or wide surfaces, you can make your own guide just as you would for a hand saw.

Table saw and radial-arm saw. Two stationary power saws that are excellent for shelf building are the table saw and the radial-arm saw. These tools perform very accurately and can be a blessing for the woodworker who does a lot of cutting.

The table saw is a power circular saw that is permanently mounted in a table. Instead of the blade being moved through the wood, the wood is fed to the blade. Locking rip fences (bars that clamp across the table) and miter gauges (guides that run in slots in the table) make the table saw the most accurate saw for ripping or for crosscutting short pieces of wood. Blades can be changed to fit the job, or a combination blade can be used for general-purpose work.

TABLE SAW

The radial-arm saw is another circular saw that uses the same blade types as the portable circular saw and table saw. The wood is positioned on a table; the motor and blade, mounted on an arm above the table, are drawn across. The saw can be raised, lowered, tilted, and even swiveled for miter cuts or rip cuts. Its greatest advantage over the table saw is its ability to crosscut long pieces.

RADIAL-ARM SAW

Sawing curves and irregular lines

Unlike most blades designed for cutting straight lines, a blade for cutting curves or zigzagging, irregular cuts must be narrow in shape and used in an almost straight up-and down position. Four saws for cutting curves are discussed in this section: the keyhole saw, coping saw, saber saw, and band saw. The first two are very inexpensive handsaws; the saber saw, as already mentioned, is a most versatile electric tool; and the band saw is an expensive shop tool. All four use replaceable blades.

Keyhole saw. Also known as a compass saw, the keyhole saw is typically used in making irregular or curved cuts and in starting cuts in the center of a board or panel from a small drilled hole. Blade lengths vary from 10″ to 14″. The blade is pointed at the "toe" (tip) and is less than an inch wide at the "head."

The handiest type to buy comes as a kit, with three interchangeable blades: one cuts broad curves or straight lines rapidly; one saws tight curves, zigzags, and cutouts; and one cuts metal. The last blade, for metal cutting, is what makes the package a bargain; it saves the additional expense of buying a hacksaw. (You may have to cut metal for some shelving projects.)

When cutting curves with the keyhole saw, cut perpendicular to the surface. Be careful with the

blades; they tend to bend easily. To begin a cutout, insert the blade in a previously drilled hole. Once you've started a long, straight cut, you can insert a regular handsaw in the cut to finish the job quickly.

KEYHOLE SAW

Coping saw. With its thin, wiry blade held taut in a small rectangular frame, the coping saw makes thin, accurate cuts and follows tight curves with ease—but cutting is limited to surfaces that its relatively small frame will fit around.

Both wood and metal cutting blades can be used in a coping saw frame. For inside cuts, slip the blade through a predrilled hole and then reattach it to the frame. When cutting vertically through material held in a vise, point the teeth toward the handle and cut on the pull stroke. If you're working on something supported horizontally, as on a sawhorse, point the teeth away from the handle and cut on the push stroke.

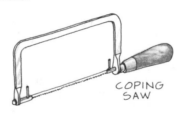

COPING SAW

Saber saw (jigsaw). Though a keyhole saw kit will get you through almost any basic curve cutting, a saber saw makes cutting curves—and, in fact, almost any cutting job—painless.

The saber saw has a high-speed reciprocating motor that drives any of several interchangeable blades to cut wood, sheet metal, plastic, rubber, leather, and even electrical conduit. Depending on how you use it, it will cut intricately curved lines, circles, straight lines, and bevels; it can even make a cutout in the center of a panel without a previously drilled starting hole.

Remember to cut with the material's good side down; the upward-cutting blade may fray the top sur-

face as it cuts. For more instructions on proper use, see the owner's manual provided with the tool.

SABER SAW

Band saw. This power saw has a continuous bandlike blade that rolls between two wheels—one above and one below the cutting platform. A narrow blade can make very tight circular cuts, and a wider, sturdier blade can cut wood over 6″ thick. Because the saw is fairly specialized, you probably won't need one for making bookshelves and cabinets—except perhaps for cutting intricately curved decorative pieces.

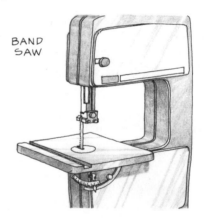

BAND SAW

Shaping

After pieces have been cut to size, minor operations such as grooving, scraping, and smoothing are often necessary before the pieces can be assembled. This is where shaping tools and techniques come into play.

Chisels have long blades squared off at the cutting end. Some have handles capped with metal, for driving with a hammer; others should be driven with a mallet or with hand pressure alone. The cutting edge of a chisel is beveled: turn the bevel up for deep cuts, down for greater control of shallow cuts.

Chisels are used for making

notches and grooves. In shelf assembly, they are most often used in cutting joints. Sold individually or in sets, chisels commonly come in ¼", ½", ¾", and 1" sizes.

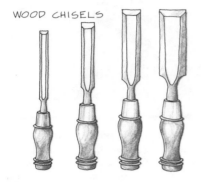

WOOD CHISELS

Planes use chisel blades set into a metal base to slice off wood at a controlled width and depth. The block plane, small enough to use with one hand, is used for fine work and for shaving end grain.

To cut end grain, use short, shearing strokes. To avoid splitting board edges, plane from the edges inward to the center of the board.

Short planes are not good for large surfaces. The shorter a plane is, the greater its tendency to ride up and down with the irregularities of a surface rather than shear them off. Bridging the small bumps, a larger plane will smooth the entire surface.

The jack plane is about twice the size of a block plane. Use the jack plane for smoothing longer surfaces, always cutting with the grain.

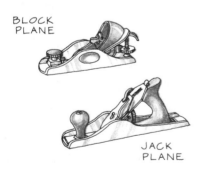

BLOCK PLANE

JACK PLANE

Angle it slightly to the direction of travel (see drawing above right), and move it forward smoothly, applying even pressure. If possible, determine how the grain slopes and cut "uphill," as shown—this keeps cuts shallow.

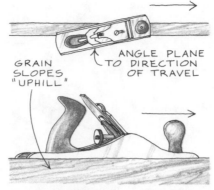

GRAIN SLOPES "UPHILL"

ANGLE PLANE TO DIRECTION OF TRAVEL

Files and rasps, abrasive tools that remove small amounts of material, are best for smoothing cuts and shaping edges. Very fine-toothed files are usually meant for filing metal and smoothing wood. Coarser rasps are designed for abrading wood rapidly. Perforated metal rasps are like cheese graters. Available in several shapes, they're useful for planing end grain and convex surfaces. They're especially good on hardboard and particle board.

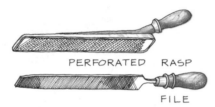

PERFORATED RASP

FILE

The electric router is a very sophisticated power tool that performs as an electric chisel, woodcarving knife, and plane. It cuts all kinds of grooves: dadoes (see page 87), V-grooves, rounded grooves, and

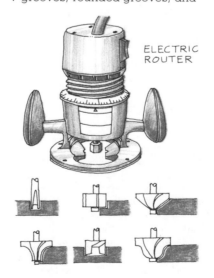

ELECTRIC ROUTER

even exact dovetails. It can round or bevel the edge of a board or finish the edge of plastic laminate at a single pass. Used with the proper cutter and template, it can whisk out hinge mortises in minutes. You'll need a router with at least one horsepower if you want to make deep cuts, such as dadoes.

Because it's a powerful, high-speed cutting tool, the router requires careful set-up and practice. Using one properly can be demanding; be sure to follow the manufacturer's instructions and recommendations.

Drilling and fastening

Drilling straight and accurately will contribute to the finished appearance of your project; proper selection and installation of fasteners are essential to its solidity and durability. Here's how to get started on the right foot.

Drilling holes

A good drill is necessary for most shelving projects. Of the several basic kinds of drill, there's sure to be one that meets your needs. Though several kinds are discussed below, you don't need them all. In fact, you can probably get by with just one: a ¼" or ⅜" electric drill. Either size is easy to use and, when fitted with the proper tool or attachment, can accomplish much more than just drilling holes.

Push drill. Used for rapidly punching small holes through wooden materials, the push drill takes bits with points that cut when rotated in either direction. A strong spring-and-spiral mechanism moves a push drill's bit clockwise as it's pushed down; some push drills also turn the bit counterclockwise when released.

Eggbeater hand drills are the standard hand drills for small holes (up to ¼"). You simply aim and crank the handle, as with an eggbeater—hence the name. These drills work on both wood and metal.

Brace and bit. For drilling larger holes in wood, there's the brace, a crank-like device that takes several kinds of bits. The three most common are the auger bit (for holes up

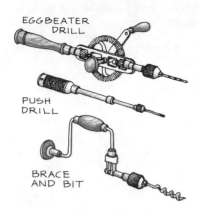

EGGBEATER DRILL

PUSH DRILL

BRACE AND BIT

to 1"), the expansive bit (adjustable to 3"), and the Forstner bit (for drilling flat-bottomed holes). Most braces have a ratchet gear, so you can bore holes even when the sweep is restricted, and they are reversible.

Portable electric drills have become standard equipment even for the casual do-it-yourselfer. They come in three sizes: ¼", ⅜", and ½". The size refers to the maximum diameter the drill's chuck will take. Though they can handle most small jobs, ¼" drills lack the power to work continuously or drive some accessories. You'll get more torque from ⅜" and ½" drills, which can handle larger bits and accessories and tougher materials. For drilling, your choices range from fractional bits, usually sold in sets ranging from ¹⁄₁₆" to ¼", to spade and expansive bits for larger holes. Special-purpose bits and other accessories are also shown; buy these as you need them. The ⅜" drill is a popular compromise between speed and power.

The best electric drills have variable-speed triggers (you squeeze harder to speed up) and are reversible. The drawing shows a typical drill and some of the many accessories available.

If you're buying a power drill, consider getting a double-insulated tool. Double insulation is designed to give you extra protection from accidental electrical shock; double-insulated tools have casings of high-impact, break-resistant, nonconductive plastic. In addition, you won't need to find an adapter for a three-pronged electrical cord plug (used to ground a tool) because double-insulated tools don't have or need the extra prong.

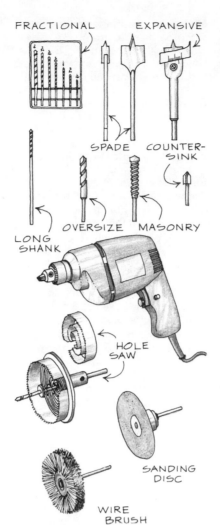

FRACTIONAL   EXPANSIVE

SPADE   COUNTER-SINK

LONG SHANK   OVERSIZE   MASONRY

HOLE SAW

SANDING DISC

WIRE BRUSH

Drill press. A fixed drill mounted on a column that in turn stands on a bench or the floor, the drill press is to the portable electric drill what the table saw or radial-arm saw is to the power circular saw. Portable drill press stands are available for electric drills (see drawing). The stands make a good compromise for the do-it-yourselfer.

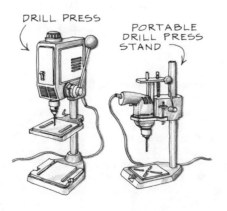

DRILL PRESS

PORTABLE DRILL PRESS STAND

How to drill properly. The three chief problems in drilling are these: 1) centering the moving drill bit on its mark; 2) drilling a hole straight; and 3) keeping the back side of the wood from breaking away as the bit pierces it. Here are some techniques for solving them.

Keep a pointed tool handy to use as a center punch in starting holes. A couple of taps with a hammer on a large nail, nailset, or punch will leave a hole that will prevent the bit from wandering.

Unless you have a drill press or a press accessory for your power drill, drilling straight holes may be difficult. Three methods you can try are shown below.

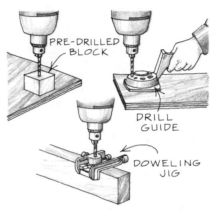

PRE-DRILLED BLOCK

DRILL GUIDE

DOWELING JIG

To keep the back side of wood from breaking away when being drilled, do one of two things: 1) lay or clamp a wood scrap firmly against your work piece's back side and drill through the work piece into the scrap; or 2) just before the drill pierces, flip the work piece over and finish drilling from the other side.

How do you know how far the drill will penetrate? You can either buy a depth gauge made for the purpose or improvise as illustrated below.

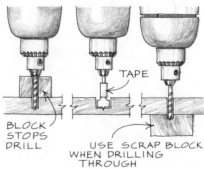

BLOCK STOPS DRILL

TAPE

USE SCRAP BLOCK WHEN DRILLING THROUGH

Here are a few general tips. Clamp materials down, particularly when using a power drill—the torque of a drill (especially when combined with a large spade bit, expansive bit, or hole saw) can easily wrench the wood out of your grasp. Hold the drill firmly.

When possible, adapt the drill speed to the job. As you drill, use generally light pressure, letting the bit do the work; excessive pressure and speed overheat the drill, make it hard to control, and ruin bits. As a general rule, avoid using bits wider than the diameter of the chuck, unless drilling softwood.

To avoid breaking small bits, don't tilt the drill once it has entered the wood. Leave the motor on as you remove the bit from the wood.

Wear plastic safety goggles, especially if you're drilling through brittle surfaces. Most manufacturers provide a valuable set of safety rules from the Power Tool Institute, along with useful guidelines for equipment maintenance; be sure to read these.

Fastening tools

The tools described so far are all cutting tools of one sort or another. You'll need another group of hand tools to assemble your project. Here are the fastening tools—for nailing, driving screws, and bolting materials together.

Hammers, symbolic of the carpenter's trade, are used to drive nails through one workpiece into another. There are finishing hammers and framing hammers; mesh-faced and smooth-faced hammers; hammers with curved claws and with straight claws. The best choice for finish work is a 16-ounce hammer with a slightly convex, smooth face and curved claw. Choose a hammerhead that's forged, hardened, and tempered from high-quality steel.

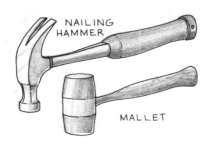

NAILING HAMMER

MALLET

Mallets, with either wooden, plastic, or rubber heads, are used to drive chisels without damaging them, to knock together stubborn joints, and to tap dowels into their holes.

Screwdrivers fall into two main categories: standard and Phillips. But there are many variations in size and length. It's important to have the right screwdriver for the job; if a screwdriver is too large or too small for a screw's slot, it can burr the screw head—or slide off and gouge the work. The Phillips head was designed to fight this problem.

You'll probably need several sizes of both standard and Phillips—but buy them as you need them. Longer screwdrivers give better leverage. Short screwdrivers are for tight spots; so is the offset type, which you crank from the side.

There are two types of ratcheted screwdrivers. One has a spiral ratchet; the blade turns as the handle is pushed in. The other type has a wide, sometimes ball-shaped handle containing the ratchet mechanism. Both types accept several different kinds of bits, and both are reversible.

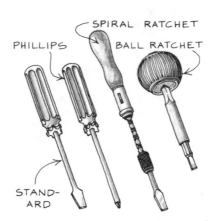

SPIRAL RATCHET

BALL RATCHET

PHILLIPS

STAND-ARD

Drill bits with screwdriver blades are energy-savers when you're driving lots of screws. Electric drills with reverse gears will back screws out, too.

Adjustable wrench. Bolt heads are usually square or hexagonal, demanding a wrench to turn them. An adjustable wrench has jaws that open and close to fit bolt heads of all sizes. Often you'll need two wrenches when tightening bolts—one to grip the bolt head, and one to hold the nut behind.

Ratchet and socket set. A more sophisticated system for turning bolts, the ratchet and socket set has one important function in shelving construction: because the socket grips a bolt from above, not from the side, it's essential for countersinking bolt heads (driving them below the work surface).

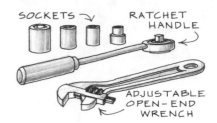

SOCKETS

RATCHET HANDLE

ADJUSTABLE OPEN-END WRENCH

Nails

The easiest way to join two pieces is to nail them together. The resulting joint is neither the strongest nor the cleanest, but it is the simplest. Nails hold wood by friction, making a joint that is strong enough if no direct pressure is exerted to pull it apart. For a stronger joint, use nails and glue.

Nail types. Common and finishing nails are recommended for woodworking. Common nails have wide, flat heads. Use finishing nails when you don't want nails to show; they have slender heads that can be hammered flush with the work surface, then set (countersunk) with a tool called a nailset. The remaining hole is filled and sanded.

Choose a nail two to three times as long as the thickness of the top piece of material to be joined. Whenever possible, nail through the thinner into the thicker piece of material.

COUNTER-SINK

COMMON NAIL

FINISHING NAIL

Both common and finishing nails come in sizes from 2-penny to 60-penny. What's a penny? "Penny" (abbreviated as "d") once referred to the cost of 100 hand-forged nails; 16-penny nails, for instance, were 16 cents per hundred.

Nailing techniques. Sharp nail tips split wood easily. Before driving them, blunt them with a few hammer taps.

To start a nail, hold it just below the head, between your thumb and forefinger; give it a few light hammer taps to get it going. If you miss it when holding it this way, you'll only knock your fingers away, not smash them. Once the nail is started, remove your fingers and swing more fully.

Keep the hammer face parallel to the nail head at contact. Don't hit finishing nails full-steam on the last few swings—tap the nail nearly flush and then drive it 1/16″ below the surface with a nailset.

Bent nail? Remove the offender by gripping the nail with the claw of your hammer and rocking the hammer back. Larger nails come out more easily if bent to the side and "curled out." To protect the work surface or to provide more leverage, put a piece of scrap between the hammerhead and the work surface.

Nails hold much better when driven at a slight angle. Don't place nails along the same grain line—it tends to split the grain; stagger them instead. If nails are causing recurrent splitting, drill small pilot holes for them, especially in hardwood.

Brads. For very fine finish work, or when nailing into delicate edges, try brads—similar to finishing nails but thinner. They are sized by length and wire gauge (a measure of thickness): the higher the number, the thinner the brad.

Screws

Though more time-consuming to drive than nails, screws make far stronger joints—especially when combined with glue.

Screw types. The four kinds of screws commonly used in wood are illustrated above right. Most common is the flathead, which sits flush with the material's surface. Two variations are the roundhead, which sits atop the surface, and the ovalhead, which is partly recessed. Roundheads are used in thin wood, or to attach another thin material between screw head and surface. Ovalheads are used for decoration or for attaching exposed hardware.

The fourth type of screw, the lag screw, is an oversize screw with a square or hexagonal head. Lag screws are driven with a wrench.

The flathead Phillips screw is also very common. Phillips heads are notched in a crosslike pattern to keep screwdrivers from slipping.

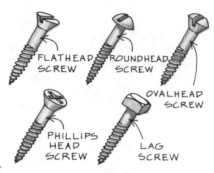

FLATHEAD SCREW · ROUNDHEAD SCREW · OVALHEAD SCREW · PHILLIPS HEAD SCREW · LAG SCREW

Three other special screws, shown below, are used for attaching units to the wall or ceiling (see page 95 for instructions). Eye screws and screw hooks secure chains or ropes that support hanging shelves. Hanger bolts leave threaded studs protruding from the wall; shelves or other units are slipped onto the studs.

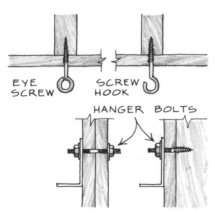

EYE SCREW · SCREW HOOK · HANGER BOLTS

Screw sizes. Woodscrews are sized by length (from 1/4″ to 4″) and, for thickness, wire gauge number (0 to 24—about 1/16″ to 3/8″).

Lag screws, with shafts from 1/4″ to 1/2″ in diameter, come in lengths from 1/2″ to 12″.

Choose a screw two to three times the length of the top piece's thickness. Screw through the thinner into the thicker piece.

Driving screws. Screws usually require predrilled "pilot" holes in all but the softest materials. Pick a drill bit the diameter of the screw's

shank, and drill only as deep as the length of the shank (to where the threads start). In harder woods, also drill a smaller hole for the threads below the shank hole; it should be about half as deep as the threaded portion is long. Use a drill bit slightly smaller in diameter than the core between the screw's threads.

In addition, flathead screws are usually countersunk to sit flush with the wood surface. This requires drilling another hole, the diameter and depth of the screw head, above the shank hole. The right countersink bit for an electric drill or manual brace will make a hole that matches the tapered contour of the screw head.

A handy electric drill accessory called a pilot bit makes pilot and countersink holes simultaneously. Some pilot bits are adjustable; others come in sets of individually sized bits. The latter are less convenient, but more durable.

If a screw is stubborn, try rubbing soap or wax on the threads. If it still sticks, drill a larger or longer pilot hole.

To drive lag screws, drill a pilot hole with a bit two-thirds the diameter and length of the screw; then start the screw with a hammer, and finish driving it with an adjustable wrench. Lag screws are commonly fitted with washers beneath the head to distribute pressure and protect the surface below.

No tool will neatly countersink a lag screw; but if a larger hole is bored, the screw head can be driven flush with a ratchet and socket. The hole is then either left open or filled with wood filler or a wooden plug.

Woodscrews can also be driven beneath the surface and covered. Cut plugs from the same type of

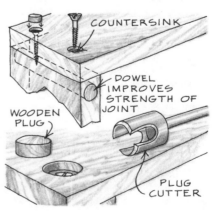

COUNTERSINK · DOWEL IMPROVES STRENGTH OF JOINT · WOODEN PLUG · PLUG CUTTER

wood with a plug-cutter (see preceding drawing) so that the grain and color will match.

Use longer screws in end grain, or insert a dowel as shown on page 85 and screw into that. Screwed joints are stronger when combined with glue, but joints without glue can be disassembled.

Bolts

Unlike a screw's tapered point—which digs into wood—bolts have uniform threaded shafts that pass completely through a material and are tightened down with nuts. Bolts are stronger than screws because the head and nut grip the material from both sides.

Bolt types. Bolts are commonly made from zinc-plated steel, but aluminum and brass bolts are available too. Some bolts are slotted for standard or Phillips screwdrivers; others are driven with a wrench. Carriage and ribbed bolts have self-anchoring heads that dig into the wood as you tighten the nut.

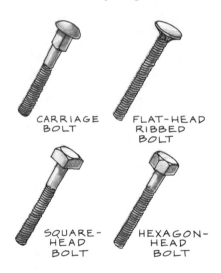

CARRIAGE BOLT   FLAT-HEAD RIBBED BOLT

SQUARE-HEAD BOLT   HEXAGON-HEAD BOLT

Bolt sizes. Bolts are classified by diameter (⅛" to ½") and number of threads per inch. Lengths run from ⅜" up; if you can't find a bolt long enough for your job use threaded rod (headless bolt shaft) cut to size, with a nut and washer at both ends.

Nuts. Hexagonal and square nuts are most common, but you'll also see wing nuts, T-nuts, and acorn nuts (see drawing). T-nuts fit flush against the surface, but are weakest.

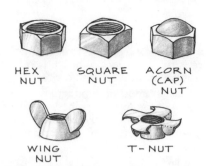

HEX NUT   SQUARE NUT   ACORN (CAP) NUT

WING NUT   T-NUT

Fastening with bolts. Most bolts take a round washer at each end of the bolt; self-anchoring bolts require only one washer, inside the nut.

To install a bolt, drill a hole through each of the two pieces you want to join; the holes should be slightly larger in diameter than the bolt shaft. Drop a washer on the bolt and slip it through the holes; then drop another washer on the end, hand tighten the nut, and tighten down the head with a screwdriver or wrench. If the nut turns on the shaft as you try to tighten it, use a second wrench to hold the nut still.

Bolts may be countersunk like screws. But if you plan to disassemble the unit at some time, don't fill the holes; you'll need access to the bolt heads to remove them, unless you use carriage bolts.

When countersinking wrench-tightened bolts, you'll have to make an oversize countersink hole and tighten the bolt with a ratchet and socket.

Pick a bolt ½" longer than the combined thickness of the two pieces to be joined. This will give the nut a firm "bite."

JOINERY

Once you've purchased your materials and measured, cut, and shaped them, you're ready to assemble your project. Joinery is the craft of assembling.

The basic joints

The most varied aspect of shelf construction, joinery is also the most demanding. The following guide to the most commonly used joints explains the use and construction of each one.

Butt joints

These are the easiest joints to make. First, square off the two ends being joined. Then butt the edge of one board against the face or end of the other, glue and clamp, and add screws or nails.

Butt joints are fairly weak unless reinforced with dowels, special fasteners, brackets, or corner blocks (see page 88).

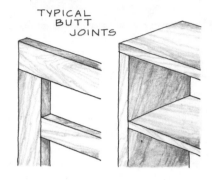

TYPICAL BUTT JOINTS

Miter joints

Two pieces cut and joined at 45° angles make up the miter joint. There are both flat and edge miters (see drawing below).

Flat miters are easier to make. They're most accurately cut with a miter box; or you can mark the angles with a combination square and then cut carefully, using a wood strip as a guide.

The edge miter is more difficult. Wide stock won't fit in most miter boxes, and it's tricky to tilt a handsaw. This is really a job for a stationary machine.

Miter joints are used for trim and for hiding end grain. They're not strong, but they can be reinforced with dowels, splines (see page 88), brackets, or nails.

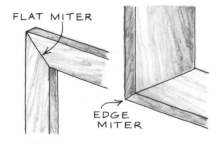

FLAT MITER   EDGE MITER

Rabbet joints

Rabbets are cut along board edges; the mating piece rests within the rabbet as shown opposite.

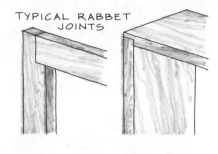

TYPICAL RABBET JOINTS

Used at corners or for recessing back pieces, rabbets help cut down visible end and edge grain; and because of the extra surface area they offer for gluing, they're very strong.

Cutting a rabbet with hand tools is a bit tricky—the goal is to make cuts as perpendicular to the board surfaces as possible. A backsaw or dovetail saw, a scrap of wood as a guide, and some type of vise or clamp will help you do the job.

First, use a combination square to mark out lines on the end, face, and two edges (see drawing). Clamp on a wood-scrap guide, lining it up with the face line, and cut to the point where the end cut will inter-

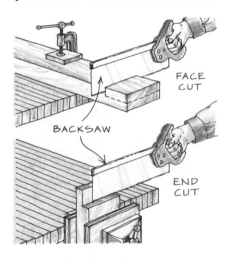

FACE CUT

BACKSAW

END CUT

sect the face cut. The end cut is the tricky one: there's no good way to clamp on a guide. Cut down carefully to meet the face cut. Clean and shape the rabbet with chisel and file.

Portable power tools make rabbets easier. An electric router equipped with a self-guiding rabbet bit will make the groove in one pass. If you have a portable circular saw, set it to the desired depth and cut along the face line first. Then make repeated passes through the waste wood. If enough cuts are made, the

Dado joints

Rabbets are made along a board's end or edge; dadoes are cross-grain grooves across a piece's face. Widely used to join horizontal shelves to uprights, dadoes are strong—the dado's lip bears the shelf weight.

Dadoes are the most difficult of common joints to make with hand tools. The hard thing is to get a groove with a smooth, even bottom.

To make a dado, first draw the border lines across the face (use the edge of the shelving material as a

TYPICAL DADO JOINTS

guide if you are making dadoes in uprights); then extend the lines around the edges, using a combination square, and connect the two edge lines at the proper depth. Now the dado is mapped out (see drawing).

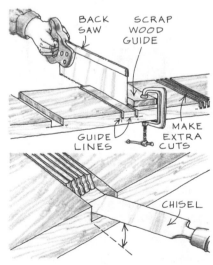

BACK SAW

SCRAP WOOD GUIDE

GUIDE LINES

MAKE EXTRA CUTS

CHISEL

Clamp on a straight piece of scrap along one face line, and cut to the right depth. Move the scrap to the other face line and repeat. If you make extra saw cuts through the waste area, chiseling will be easier

and the bottom of the dado will be more uniform.

To remove any remaining wood, use a chisel with the beveled side down, first tapping lightly with a hammer and then smoothing out the groove with several hand-held strokes.

Power tools are best for dadoes. The router, equipped with a dado bit, smooths the cut as it goes (clamp a guide onto the work for the router base to follow). There are dado blades for stationary machines and for portable power saws.

To cut dadoes with a standard power saw blade, set the blade at the right depth, cut the borders (using a guide), and make repeated passes through the waste wood until it virtually falls out. Dress each groove with light chisel strokes.

Lap joints

Overlapping construction often involves use of lap joints. Identical notches are cut in two pieces of like dimensions, and the pieces are then overlapped and fastened together.

Three types of lap joints are useful in shelving: the cross lap, the end lap, and the mid lap (see drawing below).

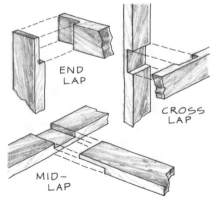

END LAP

CROSS LAP

MID-LAP

Cross laps are relatively easy to make. The width of each notch should be exactly the same as the width of the connecting piece; the depth of each notch should be one-half the thickness of the connecting piece. Cut the sides of each notch to the required depth with a hand or power saw, then cut the bottom with a chisel, coping saw, or saber saw. Smooth the cuts with a file, if necessary.

End laps are made up of two rabbet cuts that fit together. The depth of each notch should be one-half the thickness of the boards.

Mid laps are made up of a rabbet that slides into a dado notched into the connecting piece.

End laps and mid laps can be notched out with a back saw and guide, but a portable circular saw or router will ensure accuracy. See "Rabbet joints" and "Dado joints," preceding, for details.

Reinforcement

Many kinds of joint reinforcements, both manufactured and homemade, are available. All of them form strong joints alone and stronger joints when supplemented with glue.

Doweling doesn't make joints, but it reinforces them. "Through" doweling is easier than "blind" doweling. For through doweling, choose a drill bit the same diameter as the dowel, and bore slightly deeper than the dowel's length (see drawing). Make small grooves in the sides of the dowel (to allow excess glue to escape), add glue to the dowel, and tap it in with a mallet or light hammer.

With blind doweling, the dowels don't show. Instead, you mark and drill separate, matching holes in the two pieces to be joined (see drawing below). The trick is matching the holes exactly and drilling them straight. See page 83 for tips on drilling.

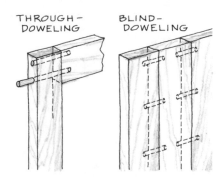

For blind doweling, try one of two methods. Either lay the two surfaces side by side and mark them as shown; then tip them on edge and drill both holes slightly deeper than ½ the dowel length. Or drill one hole, insert a dowel center (see drawing) in the hole, and press the pieces together. The dowel center,

like a tack, will mark where the second hole is to be drilled.

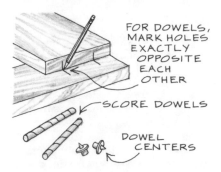

Dowels can be recessed and covered like screws or nails. They can be plugged or covered with decorative caps. They also make an attractive design detail when left visible.

Brackets and plates are made in many shapes; the most common are shown. Brackets are usually of zinc-plated steel, but some—for decorative purposes—are made of brass. In shelving, corner plates and L-brackets are useful for adding support where structural pieces meet. Mending plates are used to join pieces on the same plane (such as shelving boards joined at the edges to make wide shelves).

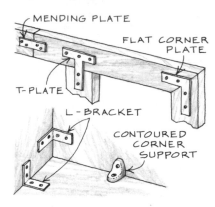

Corrugated fasteners are used at the back of miter, butt, and edge joints to reinforce glue; they can be used alone with light stock. Corrugated fasteners are simply hammered into place.

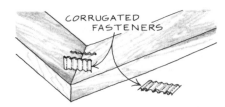

Gussets are homemade corner brackets—wood triangles fastened to the back of a right-angle joint.

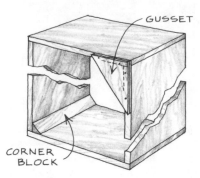

Corner blocks, or nailing blocks, are triangular or squared strips of wood placed along the inside edges of joints (see drawing above). They hold fasteners driven from outside through thinner materials.

Wooden splines are sometimes inserted in a saw kerf to strengthen miter and butt joints (see drawing).

Splines may be cut with a backsaw or dovetail saw; but they demand accuracy, so power tools are best. To be sure each set of kerfs or grooves will match, use the same table saw or router setting to cut both.

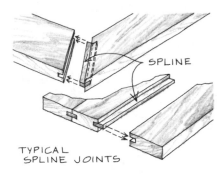

The width of the spline should be slightly less than the combined depth of the two kerfs. For most work, a good spline size is ¼" thick by 1¼" wide.

Cut the spline, spread glue along it, and place it in one of the grooves. Then push the other piece into place and clamp. When the glue is dry, trim the spline ends flush, file, and sand.

Gluing and clamping

The strength of a joint often depends on the proper application of glue.

The right glue, combined with the right clamping technique, makes a better joint than fasteners alone, and doesn't mar the work surface.

Clamps hold joints together until they dry and can be invaluable for holding shelf pieces in one place, or together, while you work on them.

Glues

A good glue, when applied and clamped properly, creates joints as strong as—or stronger than—the wood itself. There are many glues; they differ according to strength, water resistance, ability to fill gaps, and drying time. The following list covers those most useful for shelving projects.

White (polyvinyl) glue. The standard household glue, this works well on wood if firmly clamped. White glue is simple to use: apply it straight from the bottle by squeezing, and wipe the excess off with a damp rag. White glue isn't waterproof, but it resists grease and solvents. It shouldn't be used near high heat, which will soften it.

Contact cement. This glue bonds immediately on contact and requires no clamps. The initial bond is permanent, so there can be no further adjusting or aligning of parts once they are put together.

Contact cement is used primarily for attaching wood veneers or plastic laminate to wood surfaces. The older kind is highly flammable and noxious; buy the newer water-base type if you can.

Epoxy glue. Gone is the age of animal glue and heating glue in messy pots. Epoxy is extremely strong, will bond even in water, and fills gaps well.

Epoxy comes in two tubes, one tube containing resin and the other a catalyst. Because the bonding is chemical, epoxy bonds nonporous, nonwood surfaces together. Caution: don't use epoxy if you ever want to dismantle the joint. (Also, it dissolves some plastics.)

Epoxy doesn't need clamps to set, but they're still useful for aligning parts.

Resorcinol glue. Also waterproof, resorcinol is used in building boats,

and shelving that will be used outdoors—or indoors in wet, humid areas. Resorcinol bonds chemically, like epoxy, but requires clamping. It leaves a dark stain that will show through paint, so you need to be neat if you're planning a fine finish.

Clamps

Clamps serve two related purposes: they're like a second pair of hands helping to steady parts that are being assembled, and they hold joined pieces together while glue dries.

Clamps come in many shapes (see drawing). You can also—and may have to—improvise your own.

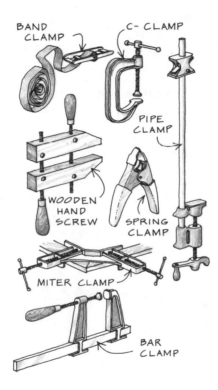

C-clamps are best for small work: clamping localized areas, holding work to a bench, and attaching scrap guides for sawing. Jaw widths range from 2" to 16".

Wood hand-screws have parallel wooden jaws that adjust for depth and angles as well as width. The jaws move up and down independently and rock forward and back on the adjusting rods. Hand-screws are useful where C-clamps can't adjust to irregularities.

Bar clamps, made in various sizes, extend over longer distances— up to 8'.

Use bar clamps for tying together large units and series of more than one joint—clamping a shelf between two uprights, for instance. They're also useful for joining wide boards at the edges.

Pipe clamps are essentially like bar clamps: you buy the clamp fittings and attach them to a length of pipe that suits your job. The attraction of pipe clamps is twofold: you can interchange pipes of various lengths, thus eliminating the need for a whole set of separate clamps; and pipe clamps are much less expensive than bar clamps.

Miter clamps are made specifically for applying pressure to both sides of a miter joint, but they're also useful any time you need to clamp two boards at a 90° angle.

Band clamps are for irregular-shaped pieces; they're wrapped around the structure to be clamped, then drawn tight—like a belt.

Gluing and clamping

Before gluing, test the fit of the pieces to be glued by assembling them dry. Make any adjustments necessary in joints at this point. Plan the assembly sequence in advance.

Pieces to be glued should be clean and dry. Spread glue evenly on both surfaces to be joined. Be careful, when using fast-drying glues, that glue already applied to one part of a large surface doesn't dry while you're working on another area.

The end grain of wood, which is usually more porous, may absorb extra glue; add a second coat.

Contact cement, applied with a serrated spreader or an old brush, is usually allowed to dry for 20 to 30 minutes before the pieces are joined.

Most glues allow for some adjustment of pieces during assembly. Check joint angles with a combination square and adjust before the glue sets. Temporary braces made of scrap wood can be tacked on to fix angles.

When clamping, cushion the clamp jaws with pieces of scrap to avoid marring the work surface. Tighten clamps until snug, but not too tight.

Use a chisel blade and a rag dipped in warm water to remove excess glue before it dries. The chisel blade will give you access to tight corners.

Working with laminate, veneer, and acrylics

Plastic laminate and veneer are used to cover less expensive types of wood, such as plywood or particle board, with a protective, decorative face. Acrylic sheets make shelves, sliding doors, and trim.

Here are basic assembly techniques for each material.

How to apply plastic laminate

Measure and mark the plastic, score the cut-off line with a utility knife, and cut—top side up with a handsaw, top side down with a circular saw. Use a low angle with the handsaw, or a fine-toothed blade with a power saw, to avoid chipping. Thin pieces can simply be scored, then bent to cut.

Check alignment before gluing. Apply contact cement to both surfaces and allow to dry for 20 to 30 minutes. Cover the wood surface with a piece of heavy brown wrapping paper, and lay the glued side of the laminate down on the paper. The glue, if dry enough, should not stick to the paper.

Align all edges, then slowly begin pulling the paper out, pressing the plastic down as you go. A roller is helpful once the laminate is attached. On large surfaces, try using two overlapping sheets of paper, and work one side at a time.

Once it's laid, laminate can be trimmed to exact size with a router bit or dressed with a fine-toothed file. If you're laminating the edges as well as the top of a surface, do the edges first and cut the top to fit.

How to apply wood veneer

Applying wafer-thin wood veneer is essentially like applying plastic laminate (see above).

Traditionally, wood veneer came in narrow sections; 12" was the maximum width, and veneering large surfaces was a game of matching seams and edges. Now there's a very thin, flexible kind of veneer, available in sizes up to 4' by 8', that is applied like plastic laminate.

The best cutter for veneer is a sharp utility knife or a veneer saw—like a comb with teeth on both sides. Use a carpenter's square or other metal straightedge as a guide while cutting. Glue with contact cement, following the instructions for plastic laminate (preceding).

After the veneer is down, roll it carefully to even the surface. Once attached, wood veneers are finished like regular wood.

Flexible wood trim, in 1" or 2" rolls, is available for veneering edges. It's made in many hardwood types.

Veneer can be trimmed with a router, file, or small (3½") trimming plane.

How to cut acrylic sheets

Acrylic plastic can be cut, drilled, and bent to various shapes. To cut ⅛" or ¼" sheets, score with a plastic scriber and slip a ¾" dowel under the cut; then press down on both sides, holding your hands about 2" from the intended break, as illustrated. For strips less than 2" wide, or for sheets thicker than ¼", use a handsaw with fine teeth or a circular saw with a carbide-tipped plywood blade.

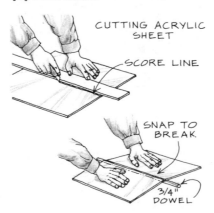

CUTTING ACRYLIC SHEET

SCORE LINE

SNAP TO BREAK

¾" DOWEL

Curved cuts can be made with a fine-toothed saber saw blade or a coping saw. Holes are drilled in acrylics at slow speeds (back the hole with a scrap to prevent chipping). Make large holes with a hole saw.

Edges can be filed, sanded, and polished with wet-and-dry sandpaper and a buffing compound.

FINISHING

Finish wood as carefully as you assembled it. A good finish keeps dirt and moisture out of wood pores and grain, wards off dents and scratches, enhances fine wood, and covers the defects in less than the best. This section tells you, in sequence, the steps to take in finishing your shelving project.

Wood preparation

Before you can finish it, the work must be carefully prepared—which means patching, sanding, and sealing.

Wood repairs. Cracks, hammer marks, and holes should be filled before sanding. This is best done with wood dough.

Wood dough is spread with a putty knife. Build each patch up above the surface slightly, then sand level. Build the patch up in layers when filling deep holes.

When choosing patching material, consider the final finish you'll be applying. If you plan to paint, the color of patches isn't crucial. But if you'll be staining, choose a patch the same color as the final finish; stain won't cover repairs the way paint will. To be sure of the best match, test the combination on a scrap of the same wood.

For a clear finish, pick a patch the same shade as the wood.

Sanding. There are three levels of sanding: rough, preparatory, and finish. For the rough stage— sanding out defects—use 80-grit sandpaper; for the middle stage— general smoothing—use 120-grit; and for the finish stage—getting a super-smooth surface—use 220-grit.

Sand either by hand or with a power sander. If by hand, buy or devise a hand block to avoid gouging the surface.

There are two main types of portable electric sanders: belt and vibrating. Belt sanders abrade wood quickly—they're useful for rough, general sanding. Vibrating sanders are better for fine sanding. The type that moves the paper back and forth is the best for finish work. Always keep a sander's movement in line with the grain.

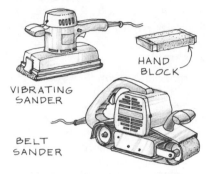

VIBRATING SANDER

BELT SANDER

HAND BLOCK

When the surface is smooth, dust the work with a brush or vacuum, then wipe the surface with a rag moistened with mineral spirits.

Sealing

A sealer is often applied to sanded wood before finish coats. Its primary function is to reduce moisture absorption so that later finish coats go on more evenly.

Shellac, diluted with alcohol, is often used as a sealer. A coat applied before staining will help prevent stain from soaking into wood grain unevenly.

Douglas fir plywood presents a special problem because the light and dark portions of the grain absorb stains at very different rates. This causes uneven coloring and often uneven swelling of the grain. Special penetrating sealers are sold to sidestep these problems.

Sealers react differently with various stains and materials; if in doubt, test the combination on a wood scrap or ask a hardware dealer.

Stains

Stain is not a finish. Used for coloring wood—to make it look aged or like another type of wood—stain also masks minor defects.

Some stains are more opaque than others; some mask or obscure grain altogether. With others, you control the tone by the amount you allow to penetrate the wood.

Pigmented oil stains are made of finely ground color pigments (similar to those used in coloring paints) mixed in a solution with tung oil, linseed oil, turpentine, or naphtha.

Probably the most popular staining product for the home craftsperson, pigmented oil stains are sold under such names as "oil stains," "wood stains," "sealer stains," or possibly "pigmented wiping stains."

Penetrating oil stains are often confused with pigmented oil stains on dealers' shelves. True penetrating oil stains are composed of oil-soluble dyes dissolved in a synthetic or natural oil-base liquid that penetrates the wood fibers.

Commonly known as colored Danish oil (tung oil colored with analine dye) or colored penetrating resin (see "Penetrating resin," below), penetrating oil stains have become very popular because they're easy to apply and they usually yield pleasing results.

Water stains, while brilliant in color and inexpensive, tend to swell wood grain and dry very slowly. One tip for dealing with swelling: wet the wood lightly with warm water and sand swollen areas flush again before staining. When you apply stain, there won't be so much swelling.

If you don't want to stain, proceed directly from wood preparation to applying a clear finish; usually a sealer is also unnecessary.

Types of finish

Choose the final finish carefully. Modern finishing materials offer you a wide range of appearances from the natural look of Danish oil to the brightest, glossiest enamel. The discussion that follows will introduce you to your choices.

Clear finishes

Clear finishes include penetrating resin, varnish, polyurethane, shellac, lacquer, and finishing oils. Each has its pros and cons.

Penetrating resin is the easiest clear finish to apply; it's a one-step finish applied to bare, prepared wood. You just brush it on, allow it to stand for half an hour, and wipe it off with clean rags.

Penetrating resins solidify inside wood pores and other cavities. The wood retains its natural feel, though the color darkens somewhat. Penetrating resins offer good protection, but not as good as some other finishes.

Varnish, probably the finish most often used, offers a combination of beauty and durability.

Varnish comes in three finishes: flat, satin (or semigloss), and gloss. Two coats are usually sufficient; between coats, use 400-grit wet-and-dry sandpaper to remove excess gloss.

Varnish is liberally applied with a brush. Stroke first with the grain, then against; then smooth out with the grain one last time. The newer, synthetic varnishes dry in 2 to 6 hours, as opposed to 24 hours for the old types. Still, there's a problem with varnish's old enemy: dust. Keep the workplace clean, and stay away while varnish dries.

Polyurethane, a synthetic finish similar in appearance to varnish, is extremely durable, as well as water and heat-resistant. It's the first choice as a clear finish when toughness is of major importance.

Shellac has a warm, subtle tone and is easy to apply. Unfortunately, it's not resistant to water or solvents. Sometimes a coat of shellac is applied for color, then covered with another finish for protection (but don't use polyurethane over shellac —adhesion is poor).

Lacquer, a fast-drying finish similar to shellac, has superior durability and hardness. However, lacquer's drying speed is a liability: it can dry before it's been smoothly brushed. To overcome this problem, lacquer is often sprayed on, but don't use spraying lacquers for brushing. Instead, use a brushing lacquer, which dries more slowly.

Before applying brushing lacquer, be sure any stain and filler are thoroughly dry. You may have to use a non-lacquer-base sealer first to keep stains and fillers from being dissolved by the lacquer.

Finishing oils give the bare look of contemporary furniture. Synthetic "Danish oil" is more durable than natural linseed and lemon oils;

applied like penetrating resin, it provides a similar finish.

Enamels

For bright, solid colors—and for masking lower grades of wood—choose an enamel: traditional oil-base, acrylic-base, or polyurethane. Colored enamels are basically varnish with pigments added.

Enamels come in flat, semigloss, and gloss (acrylic is not available in gloss). Apply them with a brush, like varnish. To seal bare wood, an enamel undercoat is usually applied before the finish coat. Acrylic will require more coats than oil-base. Sand the undercoat, then lightly sand each finish coat with 220-grit paper. The more coats you apply, the lighter the sanding required. The final coat is not sanded.

Oil-base covers better than acrylic and is more durable.

Acrylic-base (latex) dries fast and cleans up with warm water.

Polyurethane is the toughest of the three; use it for the greatest resistance to abrasion.

BOXES, DOORS & DRAWERS

Shelf units become multipurpose wall systems with the addition of basic cabinetry: boxes, doors, and drawers.

A simple box will greatly expand the flexibility of your shelving system. The box can serve as a desk, wine rack, record bin—just about anything you want. Add adjustable shelves using tracks and clips (see page 16) to further increase storage or organize contents. The addition of doors and drawers will increase its usefulness even more.

The basic box

Regardless of size, shape, or purpose, there are only a few ways to build a box. The discussion below

details several easy approaches, using three of the basic joints discussed on page 86. Later sections show you how to add doors and drawers to the basic box for increased flexibility.

Materials

Plywood is the strongest, most stable material for wall system boxes. Use ordinary softwood plywood and paint or stain it, or cover it with an attractive veneer (see page 90 for veneering techniques). Hardwood plywood makes beautiful wall system boxes, but is expensive. Particle board works well, but is not as attractive (painting is a good idea with particle board). Of course, you can use solid wood; but remember that its maximum width is about 12"—unless you join boards at the edges, which requires either blind doweling or spline joints (see page 88). Whatever the material, the basic joinery involved is the same.

Joinery

The drawings below show basic ways of putting together a box. Of these, the rabbet joint is the strongest, since there is some interlocking of parts and a greater contact area for gluing than in the butt joint. The butt joint, however, is quite satisfactory if it's carefully made, and especially if you put a back in the box.

Miter joints work for boxes, especially small ones, but they don't

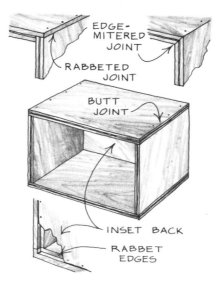

EDGE-MITERED JOINT

RABBETED JOINT

BUTT JOINT

INSET BACK

RABBET EDGES

have much strength. In addition, power tools are almost a must for accuracy; there is no convenient way to make the necessary edge miters with hand tools.

If you elect to install a back, ¼" plywood is a good choice. Plan to rabbet the rear of the box to receive the back, if possible; this makes for strong, attractive construction.

Assembly

Measure, mark, and cut your materials according to the directions on pages 78 and 79. Assemble the parts, using glue and nails, screws, or dowels (see pages 84–85 and 88).

Stand the two shorter sides on your work surface and join them to one of the longer sides. Then turn the whole unit over and add the fourth side; use a combination square to square everything before the glue sets. Finally, glue and nail on the back. If you're not putting on a back, attach a temporary brace or a miter clamp to hold the box square while the glue dries.

Doors

Plywood, hardboard, acrylic sheets, and glass make good doors for wall systems. Solid lumber is too heavy and tends to warp, and all but rather narrow doors require that several pieces be joined at the edges.

Doors fall into several categories: flush, overlapping, lip, drop, and sliding. The first four are attached by hinges; sliding doors follow grooved tracks.

Hinged doors

Flush doors are set inside the edges of a unit. They must be cut exactly to size (allow ¹⁄₁₆" space on all sides for clearance).

Overlapping doors sit in front of a unit; they're easy to install and more forgiving of errors in alignment. Lip doors are similar, but the inside edges are grooved (rabbeted) or beveled to inset slightly. You can also fashion a lip by gluing a smaller plywood piece on the back of the door face (see drawing opposite).

Drop doors open by swinging down, and with proper support can

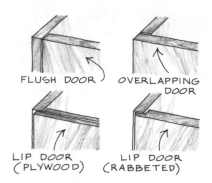

FLUSH DOOR   OVERLAPPING DOOR

LIP DOOR (PLYWOOD)   LIP DOOR (RABBETED)

double as table or desk surfaces, as shown below.

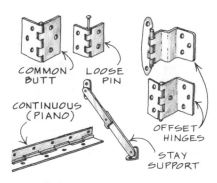

DROP-DOWN DOOR

Hinges. Hundreds of shapes and sizes are available. The most useful for cabinet doors are shown in the drawing below.

Butt hinges are the most common; the ones with pins allow you to remove the door without unscrewing the hinges.

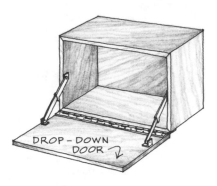

COMMON BUTT   LOOSE PIN

CONTINUOUS (PIANO)

OFFSET HINGES

STAY SUPPORT

Offset hinges are designed for overlapping and lip doors; they also help you avoid having to fasten into plywood edges. Continuous (piano) hinges are best for drop doors. They're available in lengths to 6'; you cut them to exact size with a hacksaw. Stay supports check drop doors from opening too far, and allow them to be used as desks and work surfaces. Chains will work, too.

Installing hinged doors. Cut the door to size (see page 79 for tips on cutting). Flush doors must be especially accurate. Check the corners for square and adjust as necessary with a block plane.

When you install butt or continuous hinges, insert paper matches or similar spacers between the two pieces to be joined. This will allow proper clearance so the door can operate.

Flush doors should be wedged all the way around during installation —again, use paper matches. The hinges can be screwed to the outside face, or recessed so that only the pins show (see "How to cut a mortise," below). Prop the door in the space, then mark both the door and the case for hinge placement. Attach the hinges first to the door and then to the case.

Overlapping and lip doors can be mounted with the unit on its back. Use wedges to space the door away from the cabinet.

How to cut a mortise. A mortise is a recess cut out so that a hinge (or other piece of hardware) can be installed flush with the wood surface. The technique is similar to cutting dadoes with a chisel.

Mark the outline of the hinge, and score the lines, first with a sharp knife and then with light taps on a chisel, always keeping the bevel of the chisel facing waste wood. Score the edge of the door or case to the proper depth, also. Then make a series of parallel cross-grain cuts to the depth mark, as shown. Lower the angle of the chisel, and using hand

MAKE A SERIES OF PARALLEL CUTS

THEN CHIP OUT WASTE WOOD

pressure only, chip out the waste wood. Smooth from the side, holding the chisel almost flat. Test the fit and adjust as necessary.

Sliding doors

Sliding doors run on tracks grooved in wood, or edged by wood strips, or manufactured from metal and plastic. The manufactured types, though more expensive, are much smoother. Acrylic sheets, glass, and hardboard make good sliding doors.

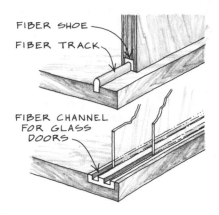

FIBER SHOE

FIBER TRACK

FIBER CHANNEL FOR GLASS DOORS

Catches and knobs

Cabinet doors need stops or catches. A simple wood strip can stop a door, but a more sophisticated catch will prevent doors from swinging both ways. Magnetic and friction catches are the most common types; magnetic catches are less dependent on strict alignment and do not wear out.

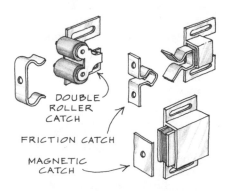

DOUBLE ROLLER CATCH

FRICTION CATCH

MAGNETIC CATCH

An endless array of knobs and pulls is available, and you should be able to find something to suit the style of any project. Some screw on, and some bolt through the door or drawer. Flush knobs (designed for sliding doors) and flush pulls must be mounted in holes or mortises. For some projects, a simple hole will make a handsome, serviceable pull.

Don't forget to apply the finish to the unit before attaching the hardware, not after.

Drawers

Drawers can really expand storage capacity. Though you can buy premade drawers in standard sizes at home-improvement centers, and design cabinets to fit them, making your own drawers is more challenging—without being too difficult. You get just what you need and save money in the process.

Materials

Drawers are best made from plywood and hardboard. Solid wood tends to warp, leading to stuck drawers, though it is often used to decorate drawer fronts. Plywood is strong for its weight and resistant to warping; thin but rigid, hardboard makes strong drawer bottoms. Use ¾" stock for drawer fronts and ½" or ⅝" for sides and backs. Use the thicker plywood for the sides if you plan to cut dadoes for the drawer bottom or slides. Hardboard bottoms are usually ¼" thick.

Drawer construction

Drawers can be built using either hand or power tools. Two versions are shown, one for each set of tools, hand and power.

A drawer built with hand tools is essentially a specialized box, made with butt joints for ease of assembly. You'll need a saw, hammer, tape measure, clamps, and glue to put it together.

Assemble the drawer shown at top right by first gluing and nailing the two front panels together; then attach the two sides to the inside front panel. Next, fit the back into the sides and nail and glue it in place.

Flip the assembly upside down and square it up with a combination square; then attach the bottom to the sides, back, and inside front panel. If you want to reinforce the bottom, cut it to fit inside the drawer and attach cleats, as shown. Then glue

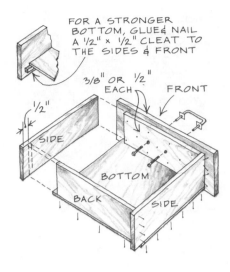

and nail the bottom to the top of the cleats.

Clamp all joints so that they'll dry square and strong.

A drawer built with power tools can take advantage of the more sophisticated joinery these tools make possible. The drawer shown requires rabbets and dadoes (pages 86–87). You'll need a power saw (portable circular, table, or radial-arm), hammer, nails, glue, and clamps. A router is also helpful.

Cut the pieces to required sizes and check for square. Cut rabbets and dadoes in the front and sides, as shown.

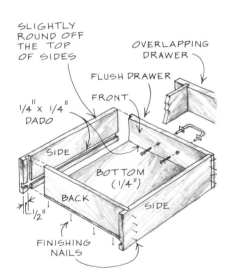

Turn the drawer front upside down and fit the bottom into place. Slip the side dadoes over the bottom, and glue and nail the sides to the front. Next, slip the back piece

between the sides and on top of the bottom piece. Check for square and nail through each side into the back.

There are two ways to attach the bottom. One method is simply to glue and nail all joints as usual. The other is to set the bottom into the side dadoes and below the back, nailing through the bottom into the back with a few small nails. This way the bottom "floats" with room to swell and contract.

Drawer guides

Drawer measurements will differ with the type of guides used. Always decide on guides before building the drawer.

Lightweight drawers that are not too wide can slide in and out without guides. But wider, heavier drawers should have guides of some type. Manufactured guides are smoothest, easiest to work with, and the most expensive. Install these according to manufacturer's instructions.

Homemade versions usually consist of a runner and guides. Several alternatives are shown in the drawing below. The runner can be a strip of wood, and the guides can be dadoes cut either in the drawer sides or in the cabinet sides. Alternate guides can be made of strips of wood, as shown; or you can buy ready-made plastic channel to serve as guides.

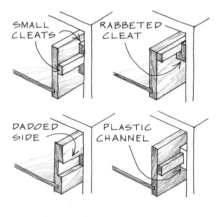

Drawer substitutes

For storage, there are many substitutes for drawers. Molded plastic tubs, wire baskets, produce crates of plastic or wood, and even baking pans are usable. Design a frame they'll slide into, and they become instant drawers.

INSTALLING YOUR PROJECT

No project is finished until it's installed. Does it need to be attached to a wall, ceiling, or floor? The type of surface will dictate the kind of fastener needed; hollow walls and solid masonry walls, for example, warrant different approaches.

Fastening to walls and ceilings

Most house walls and ceilings are not solid; they're built of sheet materials laid over a framework of studs and joists (see drawing at right).

Wall studs are structural members, usually of 2 by 4 lumber, that run vertically at regular intervals between a sole plate at the floor and a top plate. Ceiling joists run horizontally above the studs to frame the ceiling or upper-story floor.

Common sheet materials include gypsum wallboard, plaster (with wooden lath or wire backing), and paneling. These materials alone will not hold much weight.

In contrast, masonry walls, which are solid, will hold plenty of weight. With them the problem lies in attaching the fastener itself.

How to find studs and joists

Studs and joists are spaced, according to building codes, at regular intervals—usually 16″ or 24″. Once you've found one stud, locating the rest should be easy.

There are several methods for finding the first stud. From one of the four major corners of a standard house, try measuring in 14½″. If you find the first one there, the next studs should be at 16″ intervals.

Paneling and wallboard often show where nails have been driven into studs and joists. If nails don't show, use a stud finder, an inexpensive device that has a magnetized needle that dances as it nears a nail head.

If you're still uncertain, make exploratory holes in a likely but inconspicuous spot with a small drill.

The same methods apply to finding joists. If the ceiling is suspended, push up a section and look for solid wood. If you're working on the top (or only) story of the house, you may have access to an attic or crawl-space where the joists are exposed.

If necessary, studs and joists can be bridged with crossmembers (see drawing below), and the shelving unit secured anywhere along the bridge with nails or woodscrews.

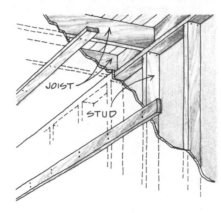

Wall fasteners

If anchoring into the house framing isn't practical, or if you're dealing with a masonry wall, you can still attach your shelves securely.

Spreading anchors, consisting of a bolt and a metal sleeve, are pushed through a hole or tapped into the wall. Tightening the bolt expands the sleeve against the wall's back side. The bolt is then backed out, slipped through the fixture to be attached, and tightened in the sleeve again.

Toggle bolts have spring-loaded, winglike toggles that expand once they're through the wall. Drill a hole large enough for the toggles when compressed, then pass the bolt through the fixture to be mounted. Slide the toggles through the hole—they'll open on the other side and pull up against the back of the wall when the bolt is tightened.

Plastic anchors expand inside the hole itself; they're not as strong as either spreading anchors or toggle bolts, but they can be removed.

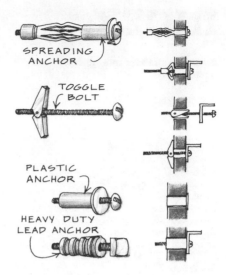

Expanding anchors for masonry walls are lead, plastic, or fiber sleeves with a hollow core for bolt or screw. Drill a hole the diameter of the sleeve and slightly longer than it, and tap the sleeve in. Slip the bolt or screw through the fixture to be attached, and drive it into the sleeve. Use lag screws or machine bolts for greatest strength.

Gauging level and plumb

When you're attaching shelving to a wall, floor, or ceiling, a couple of handy tools can help you ensure that the shelves are level and the uprights plumb.

The spirit level accurately shows both level and plumb. A glass tube at the tool's center indicates level when an enclosed air bubble lines up between two marks. Similar tubes at each end indicate plumb. The standard spirit level is 24″ long.

A plumb bob provides another way to gauge plumb—by gravity. It's nothing but a pointed weight at the end of a string. When the other end of the string is fixed and the weight hangs free, the line of the string will show perfect plumb.

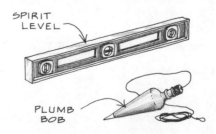

INDEX

Boldface numbers refer to color photographs.

Photographers

Clyde Childress: 66 left. **Richard Fish:** 43 top, 45 top, 52 top, 55 left, 64 bottom. **Jack McDowell:** 12, 13 top, 14 left & bottom, 15, 19 right, 20 top, 22, 23, 25, 27 bottom, 28 bottom, 30 right, 39, 41 top, 42 top, 43 bottom, 44 bottom, 46, 48, 49 top, 51 top, 54, 55 right, 56 right, 58, 59 top left & bottom, 63 bottom, 64 top, 66 right, 67, 68 top left & bottom, 70 right, 71, 72. **Steve W. Marley:** 10, 24 bottom, 26, 28 top, 29 top, 50 top, 52 right, 62 left, 63 top. **Jim Peck:** 68 top right. **Merg Ross:** 42 bottom. **Rob Super:** 11, 13 bottom, 14 top, 18, 19 left, 20 bottom, 24 top, 27 top, 29 bottom, 30 left, 38, 40, 41 bottom, 44 top, 45 bottom, 49 bottom, 50 bottom, 51 bottom, 52 bottom left, 56 left, 59 top right, 62 right, 70 left.